Stories of

Archer Wallace

Alpha Editions

This edition published in 2024

ISBN : 9789362928757

Design and Setting By
Alpha Editions
www.alphaedis.com
Email - info@alphaedis.com

Contents

INTRODUCTION

If you are the sort of a boy who is afraid of becoming dissatisfied with his present outlook on life and vision of possibilities for the future, you had better not read this book.

In fact, there are just two classes of boys who should be permitted to read these fascinating pages.

The ambitious boys are in one class; those who are determined to make their lives count. That type of boy will be helped toward finding the best outlet for his services. He will learn of fields of investment for his life work which have brought rich returns to other boys. His vision will be broadened, his objective made higher.

The other class of boy who should read this book is that in whom the fires of ambition have not yet been kindled; he who is living on the dead level of life, just "groping to and fro". This type of boy will be inspired to tackle the climbing life when he learns of the handicaps which other boys have overcome and of the great goals they have won. The following lines from the story of Edward Bok, the little Dutch boy, is descriptive of general conditions: "When he got out into the world, he was astonished to find how many of his young friends believed that the only way to get on was through favouritism. That was not his experience. He found that if a young man were willing to work and do his very best, the way to success was wide and it was not overpeopled. He was astonished to find how many young men there were who were not doing their best or anything like it. He did all that was expected of him and a little more."

As boys, we resent "being nagged at". We rebel, and our souls shrivel up when Dad, Mother, Teacher or some interested friend starts to point out our weaknesses. On the other hand, how it stirs our blood and thrills us as we read of some fellow who has played the game of life against fearful odds and has come through with a crowning achievement!

Some one has said, "He can who thinks he can." No boy can read these "Stories of Grit" without believing more firmly in his ability to succeed.

When the grind comes and we are ready to give up the struggle, the inspiration from these "boys who overcame" will send us both to our little difficulties with an enthusiasm which knows no defeat.

I have talked with boys who have said "Latin has me licked", and they were ready to throw over the possibilities of a college course and a chosen profession because of the Latin in the Matriculation Examination. Give any boy one hour with these "Stories of Grit", and I guarantee that it will stiffen his backbone and give him a punch so effective that he will be able to "lick his weight in wildcats".

TAYLOR STATTEN.

CHAPTER I.
THE BLIND BOY WHO BECAME POET, PREACHER AND AUTHOR.

George Matheson was born in Glasgow, Scotland, on March 27th, 1842. When he was only eighteen months old his mother made the melancholy discovery that his eyesight was defective. He had inflammation at the back of the eyes. Several specialists were consulted, but little hope was held out to the boy's parents.

The failure of his eyesight was gradual. For several years he could see fairly well. During the greater part of his school-life he could read and write by using powerful eye-glasses and large type. He was permitted to sit near the window so that he might get the full benefit of the sunlight. In spite of the serious difficulties which faced him during those years, George Matheson took high standing in his class. He managed to learn French, German, Latin and Greek, and in some subjects he led his class.

He was ever hoping that his eyesight would improve. It was the custom of his family to spend most of their summer holidays at one of the seaside resorts on the Firth of Clyde, and George took great delight in watching the steamboats as they plied up and down the river. It was there that he spent many anxious hours testing his eyesight. He would stand on the pier and watch the boats in the distance. He would try to make out how many funnels each had, and as they drew nearer, what their names were. At times he thought that his eyes were improving; but at last he had to admit to himself that they were gradually getting worse.

For the greater part of his life he was largely dependent upon other people. His lessons at college were read to him, and, thanks to a marvellous memory, he learned with amazing thoroughness. He had a wonderfully cheerful disposition. To become blind when so young would have been sufficient to crush all brightness out of most lives, but not so with George Matheson. He rose above his terrible calamity, and showed himself a real hero.

When only eleven he was admitted to the Glasgow Academy. He took his place alongside other pupils, studied the same subjects, and sat for the same examinations. When it came to marking his exam. papers no favours whatever were granted to him, and yet his four years at the Academy were years of unbroken distinction. In his first year he gained the prize for history and religious knowledge. In his second year he gained prizes in

Latin, history, geography and English composition. In his third and fourth years he won nearly all the special prizes, and finished with a wonderfully high record.

He matriculated for Glasgow University in 1857, when he was only fifteen. During his term there his eyesight became gradually worse, until by the time he was eighteen he was practically blind. When this terrible handicap is taken into consideration, George Matheson's record at the university stands as a wonderful example of perseverance and pluck. In all his classes he stood high, and especially shone in debates and oratorical contests. He received his B.A. degree in 1861, with "honourable distinction in philosophy," and his M.A. degree one year later. In 1862 he entered Divinity Hall to study for the ministry. For four years he gave himself to the most careful preparation for that calling, and in 1866, after nine years spent in Glasgow University, he was licensed to preach.

In January, 1867, George Matheson became the assistant minister at St. Bernard's parish in Glasgow. He preached regularly to large congregations, and prepared his sermons with much care. When he stood up to preach people forgot all about his blindness. He committed the whole service to memory; hymns, lessons, and sermons, and such was his splendid memory, that he never seemed at a loss for anything to say. After a year at St. Bernard's he was appointed minister of Innellan Church, where he remained for several years and preached and ministered to a very large congregation. Innellan, because of its beautiful situation and bracing air, had become a favourite summer resort, and to these attractions was added George Matheson's fame as a preacher. People came from far and near to hear him, and none ever went away disappointed.

What a picture it is to think of that blind man, standing there in his pulpit, instructing and comforting people who had perfect eyesight and seemed more favoured than he. Yet in all his sermons and in his conversation, there was cheerfulness and gratitude to God. No one ever heard him murmur or complain, and when he stood up and offered prayer, or read the Psalms in his clear, ringing voice, everyone realized that his whole heart was in the service. He became known as "Matheson of Innellan" and many people went there, summer after summer, in order to hear him preach.

In 1886 George Matheson was called to St. Bernard's Church, Edinburgh. In May of that year he began his work as minister to that congregation, and remained for thirteen years. It was a very large congregation. There were nearly fifteen hundred members, in addition to hundreds of others who were simply attendants.

Dr. Matheson resolved that he would not only preach to his people, but would visit them in their homes. His sister was deeply attached to him, and accompanied him wherever he went. Before he had been six months at Edinburgh he had visited six hundred families, besides calling upon the sick, the aged, the infirm and the dying. In addition to all this he was preparing sermons of rare quality and working in close sympathy with all the associations of his church. The visits he made upon his people were occasions long to be remembered. He was so warm-hearted and full of sympathy, that every person he met realized that it was no formal visit. Dr. Matheson kept up this method of visitation throughout his whole ministry. His church grew until there were nearly eighteen hundred members; yet he made a determined effort to keep in close touch with them all; and, blind though he was, he succeeded much better than most men would have done who had perfect vision.

Like Henry Fawcett, the blind Postmaster-General of England, Dr. Matheson had a marvellous memory. No doubt the loss of eyesight does much to quicken the faculty of memory. Often after he had preached, the vestry would be besieged with people who were anxious to speak with him. Many of these people had known him before, and it was a source of amazement to them to have the blind preacher call them by name almost immediately after hearing them speak. Sometimes visitors from a distance, whom he had not seen for many years, would say, "You'll not remember me, Doctor." Perhaps a puzzled look would cross his face; then he would say, "yes I do; you are Mackintosh, of ——" It would be Mackintosh right enough, and Mackintosh would be a very much surprised man.

In addition to his preaching and visiting, George Matheson was the author of many fine books. In 1882 he published a book of meditations with the title "My Aspirations". The success of this book was instantaneous, and in a very short time the entire edition was sold out, and several other editions followed. Later he published many other volumes, among them being: "Moments on the Mount", "Voices of the Spirit", "Searching in the Silence", "Times of Refreshing", "Leaves for Quiet Hours", and "Rests by the River". His books proved helpful to thousands of people. From every part of the world letters came from people whose lives had been greatly blessed by reading the works of the blind author. What was true of his preaching was also true of his writing. People felt, at once, the strong, cheerful, grateful heart of the author. Great numbers of people, around whose lives heavy clouds had gathered, had their hearts strengthened, and their faith in God renewed, as they read George Matheson's books.

In 1882 he wrote his famous hymn, now known the world over, "O Love, that will not let me go." It would be impossible to tell just what this hymn has meant to thousands of people. The hymn is now found in most hymnals and has become a great favourite. George Matheson gives the following account of how he came to write it; "The hymn was composed in the manse of Innellan on the evening of the sixth of June, 1882. I was at that time alone. It was the day of my sister's marriage, and the rest of the family were staying over night in Glasgow. Something had happened to me, which was known only to myself, and which caused me the most severe mental suffering. The hymn was the fruit of that suffering. It was the quickest bit of work I ever did in my life. I had the impression of having it dictated to me by some inward voice rather than of working it out myself. I am quite sure that the whole work was completed in five minutes, and equally sure that it never received at my hands any retouching or correction."

George Matheson lived to be sixty-four years of age and managed to fill every hour with useful and loving service. To read an account of one day's work in the life of this blind man is sufficient to make most people realize how hard he worked. He was methodical in his habits and careful to leave no duty undone. After breakfast each morning he attended to his correspondence, generally answering letters by return mail. Then he would have read to him the morning papers. He showed a keen interest in everything that was going on. From that he would pass on to his studies in French and German. This would be followed by some study in science, philosophy, history or theology. Then he would dictate to his secretary, something for the press or for his own use as a speaker. Added to such work, of course, there were his extensive labors as pastor and preacher, and it can be truthfully said that he did not fail in anything. Whatever task he put his hand to, he did with all his might.

George Matheson died at North Berwick, on August 28th, 1906, and was buried at Glasgow a few days later. Tributes of sympathy came to his relatives from all over the world. By his strong preaching, and probably still more by his brave, cheerful spirit as set forth in his books, he had helped a very great number of people everywhere. In his noble hymn he had written, "I trace the rainbow through the rain." That is exactly what he did. Where so many others saw only difficulties, he saw possibilities. And so it came to pass that, though he lived in darkness for nearly half a century, he served God and his fellow-men with a devotion which will never be forgotten.

CHAPTER II.
HOW A LAME BOY BECAME THE WORLD'S GREATEST POTTER.

In the summer of 1730 a little lad was born at Burslem in Staffordshire, England. There was no fear of the little fellow being lonely for he came into a family where there were already twelve boys and girls. Josiah Wedgewood, for that was the boy's name, was number thirteen. Was he unlucky? Well, in some ways he was, but in others he was not. His mother had her hands full with so large a family, but she taught Josiah to read and write and then sent him to a dame's school. Later he was sent to a school in Newcastle-under-Lyme. This school was three and a half miles from where he lived, but the little fellow was keen to get an education and cheerfully trudged the seven miles to and from school each day. He was a lively boy, fond of all kinds of sports and a general favourite at school. He showed a remarkable faculty for making paper designs. With pen and scissors he cut out designs of an army in combat, a fleet of ships at sea, a house and gardens, and many other interesting things. This gift of Josiah's gave great pleasure to his little friends, but the schoolmaster took a very different view and rather severely admonished the budding designer. Josiah was also fond of collecting fossils, shells and beautiful things which he found around the country lanes. He was constantly bringing these things home, and at last he fitted up a disused workshop of his father's and it served the purpose of a miniature museum.

When Josiah was nine years of age his father died. It was a great blow to the family, for while the father had never been more than an ordinary workingman, he had kept his family in fairly good circumstances. Josiah was taken from school at once and sent to help in the factory, where his eldest brother, Thomas, was in charge. For several generations the Wedgewoods had been potters and the whole countryside was famous as the chief centre of the industry in England. It was a proud day for Josiah when first he began to work at the trade in which he was destined to become so great. He was too young to understand what a serious handicap it is to be sent out into the world with little education, and besides, in those days, comparatively few received a thorough training in school. Several of his brothers and sisters never learned to read or write, and after they became men and women, they had to sign their names with a mark, for they had never learned to write even their own names.

When he was eleven a serious misfortune befell Josiah; one which darkened his whole life. The terrible scourge of small-pox swept over England, as it did over all European countries from time to time, and he suffered a severe attack. In those days medical skill had not developed very much, and the doctors were quite unequal to the task of dealing with the dreadful disease. Besides that, the utter lack of sanitation, and the conditions under which most of the people lived, were such that it seemed as though plagues must just run their course. Severe cases of small-pox were almost regarded as hopeless, and recovery was very rare. For a time it seemed as though Josiah could not live, but at last he rallied. His right knee, however, was seriously affected, and for the remainder of his life he was a cripple.

When only fourteen years of age Josiah was formally apprenticed to his brother. He had, like other apprentices, to sign an agreement that he would not gamble, frequent taverns, or indulge in any of the prevailing vices. Many boys, of course, signed such agreements without really intending to live up to their vows, but Josiah lived up to his pledge. Throughout the years of his apprenticeship he devoted himself with amazing concentration to his trade. There was a great deal of drunkenness and gambling and other vices at that time, but Josiah's record was beyond reproach. He loved his work and gave himself fully to it. Everything connected with the potter's trade he found interesting. He did not know what dull moments were.

Josiah soon showed a desire to do things in his own way. He was constantly striving after new effects and attempting new designs. Many of those working with him marvelled at his wonderful skill, but his brother Thomas did not like it. Thomas was making a fair living by doing the same old things in the same old way and he did not want any changes introduced. It seemed to him that Josiah was simply wasting his time with his new-fangled ideas. When Josiah had served his apprenticeship he offered to go into partnership with Thomas, but the elder brother was not willing, so Josiah had to look elsewhere for work.

For a while he became associated with other men and he was at liberty to make his experiments to his heart's content. But soon Josiah discovered that his associates were simply taking advantage of his good nature and profiting by his skill. In 1759, when he was twenty-nine years of age, he started in business for himself. His beginning was in a very humble way, for he had very little money; but he rejoiced in being his own master, and resolved to work away at carrying out some of the ideas he had cherished for so long.

About this time he suffered very great pain from his injured leg. At times he had to work away with his leg resting on a stool in front of him. On one occasion he injured his leg and was laid up in bed for several months.

During this period he did a good deal of reading and tried to make up for his lack of early training. He also had time to think out many new plans for his work, and he solemnly resolved to become the greatest potter of his time. His mother had died some years previously and his outlook in some ways was not very bright. He wrote in his diary: "I have my trade, a lame leg, the marks of small-pox, and I never was good-looking anyway."

When he was able to get about again he resumed his work with more enthusiasm than ever. Instead of doing as his brother Thomas and other potters were doing—simply making plain butter-crocks, brown jugs and such like, he spent a great deal of time experimenting in glazes, in a semi-transparent green color which he had made for himself. Soon his wonderfully artistic designs began to attract attention, and his reputation extended throughout England.

Up till this time practically all the really beautiful pottery in England had been imported from other countries. Because of the great distance and of the difficulties of transportation, this pottery was very expensive. An aristocratic Burnham family, who possessed some very fine rare specimens, had the misfortune to have their largest plate broken. They sought the assistance of all the leading potters to help them get a duplicate, but failed. Then they were directed to Josiah Wedgewood. He succeeded where others had failed and to the amazement of all he produced a perfect facsimile of the broken plate. The news of this achievement soon spread and he received orders for more work than he could carry out.

Some years before this, Josiah had seen Sarah Wedgewood and had become deeply attached to her. Sarah's father and his own were cousins, but whereas his father had been a humble workman, Richard Wedgewood was considered a wealthy man. By dint of hard work Josiah saved a hundred pounds, which in those days was considered quite a sum of money. He wrote to Sarah and told her of his success, and she wrote back and congratulated him, telling him how proud they were of his achievements in artistic pottery. Josiah was greatly encouraged by this letter, and on the strength of it he visited her home and asked her hand in marriage. Sarah seems to have been quite willing, but her father was very angry. He had taken a friendly interest in his distant relative, and was glad to know of the wonderful things he was doing in artistic pottery, but after all Josiah was still poor, lame, and disfigured by small-pox. He had no intention of allowing his daughter to marry such a man. He had some one else in view whom he considered would be a much better match.

It was a very painful experience for the lame man, but its bitterness was offset by one thing: Sarah herself hastened to make it clear to Josiah that she loved him and did not want to marry any one else. Encouraged by this he resolved to work harder than ever. He wrote to Sarah telling her that he would yet be the best potter that England had ever seen.

This was no idle boast. Orders for his work came so fast that he had to extend his workshop from time to time and take on more workmen. He had often noticed how untidy and slovenly the men were in the various workshops and he determined to have things done differently in his factory. Some of the men keenly resented his particular ways, but he reasoned with them, and showed them the wisdom of his methods. Soon the workmen caught the enthusiasm of their master and fell heartily in with his plans.

He determined that not one bit of poor pottery should leave his workshop. Sometimes he would look very carefully at some piece, then say, "It is good—but not good enough for Josiah Wedgewood." Then it would be destroyed. Day after day he sat with his workmen, going from one to another, rendering assistance and seeking to give to each one a very high ideal for work. He had to face great difficulties. Many of the tools in use were of no service whatever in his porcelain ware. He had often to greatly improve the tools, and in many cases invent new ones altogether. But he was not easily daunted, and his marvellous perseverance overcame all difficulties.

He was married to Sarah Wedgewood in 1764, when he was thirty-four years of age and she was twenty-nine. For many years she had been a great inspiration to him in his work and she continued to be throughout his life.

Four years after this his leg, which had seldom allowed him to have one day without pain for twenty-two years, became worse. After consultation with several doctors it was decided to have the limb amputated. There were no anæsthetics in those days by which the patient in such a severe operation could be made unconscious, and so without anything to alleviate the pain he suffered the operation. He did not shrink but bore the pain with magnificent courage. It was not his way to complain. During the twenty-two years of suffering he had very seldom said a word about his agony.

By this time Josiah Wedgewood was known throughout England and in many lands far beyond. There was great interest taken when his leg was amputated and many of the leading people of England, including the King and Queen, were greatly relieved when it was known that the operation had been a success. When he regained his strength he soon returned to the work he loved so much and sought to make his products more perfect.

Probably there has never been a more skilled potter than Josiah Wedgewood. There have been other skilful men, but they have almost always copied one from another. He followed out his own ideas. When a boy, walking several miles to and from school each day over the wide moorland, he had noticed the exquisite tints of the wild flowers. When he became a potter he copied out those same flowers in his marvellous designs. He did not copy the works of other men; he followed as his ideal the things which God had made. He was by far the most original potter that the world has ever seen. His business became one of the great industries of England and he and Sarah built an ideal village called Etruria, where they lived with their daughter Susannah, who became the mother of the famous scientist, Charles Darwin.

And so it was that the crippled boy, who left school at nine, and for long years was hardly ever a day without violent pain, became the greatest potter the world has ever known.

CHAPTER III.
THE DUTCH BOY WHO BECAME A GREAT EDITOR.

When the ocean liner, *The Queen*, docked at New York on September 20, 1870, she discharged among her passengers a Dutch family named Bok. Mr. Bok, the father, had once been in fairly good circumstances, but unwise investments had left him quite poor, so he and his wife decided to leave Holland, and with their two boys, William and Edward, start over again in the United States.

The younger boy, Edward, was not quite seven years of age. Within a few days of landing he and his brother were sent to a public school in Brooklyn. It seemed a hard beginning, for neither of the boys knew one word of English. They did not know what the other boys were talking about, nor could they make themselves understood. In their helplessness they did not have the sympathy of each other's company for they were graded according to age, and so were parted during school hours. As soon as school was dismissed the boys were each the centre of a group of tormentors, who seemed to enjoy teasing the little fellows who could neither speak, nor understand, a word of English. Edward was nick-named "Dutchy" and there was scarcely any form of cruelty which the other boys did not inflict upon him.

One day Edward was goaded into fury and turned on the ringleader among his tormentors. Much to the surprise of the big bully, and to the boys, Edward gave him a sound thrashing, and from that day on, he had the respect, at least, of his schoolmates. He learned the language quickly, and although he spoke with a Dutch accent, he adapted himself to the ways of the new country and gained confidence.

Edward's father did not find it easy to make good. He was between forty and fifty years of age and everything was new and strange. He could not find work for quite a long time and the strain began to tell upon his wife's health. Edward and his brother were quick to see how the heavy burdens were weighing upon their mother, so they decided to relieve her by rising early in the mornings; building the fire, preparing the breakfast, and washing the dishes, before they went to school. After school they gave up their play and swept and scrubbed, and helped their mother to prepare the evening meal, and wash the dishes afterwards.

One morning the boys woke up to find that there was no kindling wood or coal wherewith to build the fire, so they decided to go out each evening to gather coal which had been carelessly spilled when coal was being delivered. A good deal of wood was also lying about the streets which they were glad to get. The mother remonstrated with the boys, but Edward said: "It is all right, Mother; this is America, where one can do anything if it is honest. So long as we don't steal why shouldn't we get it?"

Money was badly needed in that home and Edward looked around to see if he could not earn something. One day he was standing looking longingly into the window of a baker's shop. The baker had just put a tray of tempting buns, tarts, and pies, in the window and he came out to look at them.

"They look pretty good, don't they?" he said, noticing the wistful look on Edward's face.

"They look all right," answered the little Dutch boy, "but they would look a whole lot better if you had your window cleaned."

"That is true," said the baker, "perhaps you will clean it."

So Edward got his first job. He cleaned that window every Tuesday and Friday afternoon, for which he received *fifty cents a week*. One day the baker was busy and Edward waited on a customer. When the baker saw how aptly he did it, he suggested that Edward help him on certain days after school and on Saturday afternoons. The salary was to be one dollar and fifty cents a week. Edward eagerly consented and hurried home to tell his parents about his rare good fortune. On Saturday mornings he took a delivery route for a newspaper, for which he received one dollar; thus he brought his weekly earnings up to two-fifty.

One evening Edward was invited to a party in Brooklyn. The thought occurred to him that the hostess would probably like to see an account of the party in the newspaper, so he wrote an account of it, giving the name of every boy and girl present, and sent it to the *Brooklyn Eagle*. The editor of the newspaper was so pleased with the idea that he offered to give Edward three dollars a column for such news. From that time Edward sought eagerly to find out where parties were being held in order to keep the editor supplied with news and to earn some much-needed money. It pleased people who had attended parties to see their names in print, and, of course, it increased the circulation of the paper. Edward was not yet thirteen, but he was attending school, working in a bake-shop after hours, serving a paper route on Saturday mornings, and acting as reporter for a newspaper.

One evening Edward learned that an office boy was wanted in the office of the Western Union Telegraph Company. The salary was six dollars and twenty-five cents a week. Edward secured the position, and so, at the early age of thirteen, he left school to make his way in the world. His mother was keenly disappointed at his having to leave school so early, but owing to the straitened circumstances of the home, she gave her consent.

Edward early developed habits of thrift. He never lost a chance of making five cents, and when he got it he did not spend it foolishly. He never used a street-car if he could walk. Thus, he was able to buy books to improve his education, and to make up for the serious handicap of having left school so early in life.

About this time he began to collect autographs. He wrote to President Garfield, Lord Tennyson, Whittier, General Sherman, Geo. W. Childs, and a great many other notables, and secured their autographs, and in several instances received friendly little letters. One day a newspaper reporter saw these letters and within a few days a long article appeared in the New York *Tribune*, giving a full account of the little Dutch boy who had secured such a remarkable collection of autographs and letters. Editors of several leading newspapers and magazines wrote to Edward and encouraged him to get into personal touch with as many distinguished people as he could, and to write brief accounts of his experiences. Thus encouraged, Edward sought and obtained interviews with President Garfield, General Grant, General Sherman, President Hayes, Mrs. Abraham Lincoln, Oliver Wendell Holmes, Longfellow, Phillips Brooks, Emerson, and many others. In every case the boy's eagerness to learn, and courteous conduct made a favourable impression and he was received with uniform kindness.

When Edward was eighteen his father died and the small amount of insurance he left barely covered the funeral expenses. Hence the two boys faced the problem of supporting their mother on their meagre income. The boys there and then determined to make their mother comfortable.

At this time he was a member of Plymouth Church, Brooklyn, where the great Henry Ward Beecher was pastor. The Young People's Society of the Church decided to publish a magazine and Edward was asked to become editor. He made a decided success of this task and before long a good deal of attention was directed to the magazine. Edward published sermons by Dr. Beecher, Dr. Talmage and others, and besides he got a number of prominent people to write for it. Readers were amazed when they opened its pages to find articles signed by the greatest people in the country. At first, the circulation of this little publication, which was named *The Brooklyn Magazine*, was small, and Edward and another boy wrapped up all the copies themselves and took them to the post office. As the circulation increased the bundles were too heavy to be carried, and a baker's cart had to be used. Before long a double-horse truck was necessary, and three trips had to be made. All this time Edward was working for the Western Union Telegraph Company in the day time and doing his editorial work in the evenings. In 1882—when, he was nineteen—he gave up his position and devoted his whole time to editing and publishing the magazine, which was now known as *The American Magazine*, and had become an important publication.

In 1884, before Edward had reached his twenty-first birthday, he was offered a position with the well-known book publishers, Charles Scribner and Sons, which he accepted. The salary was eighteen dollars a week, which in those days was considered a good salary for one so young. He astonished every one by his energy and enterprise. There wasn't a lazy bone in his body. He had an ever-willingness to work which made his success a certainty. When he got out into the world he was astonished to find how many of his young, friends believed that the only way to get on was through favouritism. That was not his experience. He found that if a young man were willing to work, and to do his very best, the way to success was wide, and it was not overpeopled. He was amazed to find how many young men there were who were not doing their best, or anything like it. They were constantly watching the clock, and afraid lest they should work one minute more than they were being paid for. When luncheon time came, Edward listened to the conversation around him and he was surprised to note that scarcely any youth ever gave a thought to anything except wages and outside interests.

Edward's idea of work was different. He resolved to do his very best and to do it every hour of the day. He did all that was expected of him and a little more. When others played, he worked, convinced that his play-time would come later. He met with many difficulties, but he overcame them with a smile. He liked fun and play just as much as any other fellow, but he felt that he ought not to take his employers' time for these things, and he felt that owing to the circumstances in his own home, it was up to him to make good.

In 1889, while he was still a young man—twenty-six years of age—he accepted the position of editor of the *Ladies' Home Journal* and moved to Philadelphia. When he took over this magazine it had a circulation of over 400,000, and so was already very well known. Under his able editorship it became one of the most influential magazines in America—and for that matter in the world. Edward Bok remained as editor for thirty years, and, under his direction, and largely owing to his great skill and hard work, the circulation grew until, when he resigned in 1919, the circulation was over *two million*.

Edward Bok was sitting one evening chatting with Theodore Roosevelt, who was at that time President of the United States. The President said, "Bok, I envy you your power with the public."

Edward Bok replied, "That is a strange remark from a President of the United States."

"You may think so," Roosevelt said, "but what you write is read by thousands when their day's work is over, and the mind is at rest. You have it on me: I envy you your power with the public." This illustrates, at least, what a tremendous influence the little Dutch boy had become in the nation, and in the world.

As editor of the *Ladies' Home Journal*, Edward Bok did a great many things which helped to make him one of the most prominent and useful citizens of the United States. He gave prizes to those who succeeded in securing new subscribers. Remembering his own lack of opportunity to secure an education, he hit upon the simple plan of giving free scholarships as premiums to the most successful canvassers. This plan grew so that nearly all the leading colleges were included, and by 1919 no less than one thousand four hundred and fifty-three free scholarships had been awarded. By this plan it was made possible for many to obtain an education who later filled conspicuous places in the business and professional world.

Edward Bok was twice asked to become American Ambassador to Holland, the land of his birth. It would certainly have seemed a wonderful thing if he could have returned in such a high position to the land he left as a poor boy, but he did not see his way clear to accept the post. He enjoyed the confidence and close friendship of such men as President Cleveland and President Roosevelt. In fact there was hardly an outstanding man in the United States with whom Edward Bok did not come into contact.

In 1918, he was invited by the British Government to join a party of thirteen American editors who were to visit Great Britain and France. On this trip he met many of the most distinguished military men and statesmen of the Allied nations. His visit to the battlefields made a great impression upon him and he was deeply moved at the courage of the Allied soldiers.

Edward Bok resigned from the editorship of the *Ladies' Home Journal* in 1919. He has since turned his attention to many things, for which his previously busy life left little room. He has been the recipient of many degrees from the great American Universities, and today, he who came to America's shores unable to speak one word of English, is recognized as a citizen of whom America may well be proud.

CHAPTER IV.
A DEAF BOY WHO BECAME A GREAT BIBLE SCHOLAR.

John Kitto was born at Plymouth, in the south of England, on December 4, 1804. His father, who was by trade a stone-mason, was a man of intemperate habits, and as a result there was constant poverty in the Kitto home. John never went to school for more than a few days in his life. At ten years of age he began to help his father and often had to stagger along under very heavy loads, or climb ladders carrying slates for the roof. For two years the boy did almost a man's work, and then, one day as he was ascending a ladder carrying a heavy load of slates, he missed his footing and fell a distance of thirty-five feet. A group of terrified workmen gathered around him and he was carried, limp and bleeding, to his humble home.

For two weeks he seemed more dead than alive. Then one day he awoke and tried to get up. He did not understand his inability to rise. When his mother came he asked for a book which, in spite of his lack of schooling, he had learned to read. His mother answered his inquiry by writing upon a slate. Then it was that the sad truth slowly dawned upon John Kitto that, as a result of his terrible accident, his sense of hearing had been totally destroyed. Several remedies were tried, but they were of no avail. The injury to the nerve of the ear was such that he could not hear any one speak, in fact he could not hear even the loudest music. Thus John Kitto, not yet thirteen years of age, found himself shut up into a world of his own in which his chief companions were books.

He was unable to help his father any longer and tried to make a little money by painting signs, such as, "Lodgings to Let". This, however, did not prove to be much of a source of income, and so his parents sent him to Plymouth workhouse, where he was taught the trade of shoemaking. When fifteen years of age he was apprenticed to a man named Bowden. This man treated the deaf boy with much cruelty. John was compelled to work hard from six o'clock in the morning until ten o'clock at night, thus working for sixteen hours each day. Even then the boy's great love for reading showed itself, for weary though he was, he spent some of the time allowed him for sleep, in poring over books. At length the cruelty of his employer became more than he could bear, so he complained to the authorities. He was released from his contract and taken back to the workhouse. There he remained for another four years, reading very eagerly the few books which were obtainable. The poor boy was practically denied companionship with other young people, not only because he was deaf, but also because, not being able to hear other people speak, he largely lost the art of speech himself. This difficulty increased as the years went by, until people who were strangers could only make out what he said with great difficulty.

His studious habits soon began to attract attention. He wrote some articles to the *Plymouth Journal* which were read with much interest. A public subscription was taken up for him in the town and he was sent to a school, that he might learn to become a printer for a missionary society.

Just about this time he came into contact with a Mr. Groves, a dentist of Exeter, who was greatly attracted to the deaf boy. He was engaged as a tutor of Mr. Groves' sons; and also several other pupils were secured for him. By this time he had become much interested in learning languages, and had mastered several, including Hebrew. Then something happened which changed everything for John Kitto. He was taken by Mr. Groves on a trip abroad, which included long sojourns in Russia, Persia, the Caucasian Provinces, and other places in the East. Four years were spent abroad, and they were great years for John Kitto. Probably the extent of his misfortune had sharpened his other faculties; at all events his observation was unusually keen and nothing escaped him. He returned to England in 1833 and wrote a series of very interesting articles for the *Penny Magazine*, signed, "The Deaf Traveller". His sojourn abroad had given him an insight into Eastern life and customs. On his return to England he decided to publish some books which would make the life of Palestine more vivid and thus increase interest in the Bible. Accordingly he published "The Pictorial Bible", in three large volumes. At that time very few books had been written with such a purpose and they were eagerly read by Bible students. Several years later—in 1845—he published his greatest work, and one which has entitled him to a foremost place among Bible commentators: "The Cyclopædia of Biblical Literature". This extensive work reveals an amazing amount of painstaking research. For a great many years it was regarded as indispensable for those who wished to closely study the Scriptures. While it is not nearly so well known now it is certain that most of the valuable material it contains has been made use of by later writers who have worked along similar lines. In addition to the foregoing books John Kitto wrote a large number of others, and also many magazine articles. Gradually his reputation spread and he became recognized as one of the great Bible scholars of his day.

He was a man of very regular habits and almost every waking moment was spent at his work of reading and writing. He rose as early as four o'clock in the morning, did a little gardening, then worked in his study nearly all day long. Several people visited him and tried to carry on some kind of a conversation, but seldom with much success. At first the method of talking by finger signs was tried, but few could understand it. Later he tried to hold some kind of intercourse by writing everything down; but this was so painfully slow that it was given up. Thus it came about that even those who wanted to help him, realized that their visits were a strain upon him and that he seemed happier when left alone.

There was one family, however, where there were several children, all of whom loved him very much. Each one of them learned to use finger signs and were never so proud as when they would carry on some sort of conversation with the great scholar. He was deeply touched by the friendship of these children, and although he could not hear them as they practised on the piano, he could feel the vibration by placing his fingers on the soundingboard and in that way marked their progress in music.

John Kitto married and had children of his own, whom he loved dearly, although he never heard them speak. In spite of the great value of his books his income was never very large at any time. In 1850 he was granted a civic pension of five hundred pounds a year. In those days that was considered a good income and no doubt it did much to lift the burden of anxiety from his mind. There certainly was no mistaking the high regard which was felt for him everywhere. Although a layman he was granted the degree of Doctor of Divinity by the University of Giessen in 1845. He was also made a Fellow of the Society of Antiquaries the same year.

In 1851 his health began to fail and some time later he went to Germany to try the mineral waters there. He did not obtain the desired benefit, however, and he died at Cannstadt in 1854, having reached the age of fifty. His passing was greatly mourned in England, for the boy from Plymouth workhouse, living for nearly forty years under a terrible handicap, had found a place of very great usefulness in the world.

CHAPTER V.
THE SLAVE BOY WHO BECAME A GREAT LEADER.

Some time about the year 1858 or 1859 a negro child was born in a log cabin in Virginia, U.S.A. The parents of the child were slaves, and utterly without education. When the child grew to be a man he could never find out the exact date, or even the year of his birth. The first things he remembered were the scenes around the squalid, little log cabin, where his earliest years were spent. The cabin itself was sixteen feet by fourteen. It not only had to serve as the sole home for the family, but was used as the kitchen for the plantation. There were no windows in it, only openings in the side which let in the light. The same openings, of course, let in the chilly air in winter. A broken-down door hung on uncertain hinges. In one corner of the miserable cabin there was a "cat hole"—a hole about seven or eight inches square—to enable the family cat to pass in or out. As there were half a dozen other holes in the cabin walls, this contrivance seemed unnecessary. There was no wooden floor to the cabin, the bare earth being considered all that was necessary. In the centre of the floor there was a large, deep hole which was used to store sweet potatoes during the winter. There was no stove in the cabin, all the cooking being done over an open fireplace.

The little negro boy—whose name was Booker Taliaferro Washington— never knew what it was to sleep in a bed. With his brother, John, and his sister, Amanda, he slept on a bundle of filthy rags on the dirty floor. The poor mother, who acted as cook to the slaves on the plantation, had little or no time to give to the training of her children, so they just grew up, and early learned to do hard work.

The family never sat down around the table together for a meal, nor was God's blessing ever asked upon the food. Like most other slaves at that time, they hardly ate like civilized beings. The children got their meals very much like dumb animals. It was a piece of bread here, and a scrap of meat there, and perhaps a potato in another place. Sometimes one member of the family would eat out of a pot, or skillet, while another would be eating from a tin plate on his knees, often using nothing but the hands to hold the food. One day, when young Booker was over at the slave-owner's house, he saw two of the young ladies eating gingerbread. It seemed to him, at that time, that the most tempting thing in the world was a piece of gingerbread, and he made a solemn vow that if ever he could afford to buy some gingerbread he would do so.

Young Booker had little time for play, in fact he hardly understood what the word meant. He cleaned the yard, carried water to the slaves in the field, and once a week took corn to the mill. This last job was heartbreaking. A heavy bag of corn would be thrown over the back of a horse, but as the horse jogged along the uneven road, often the bag would fall off, and probably young Booker would fall with it. He was not strong enough to get it back upon the horse, and so he would have to wait, maybe for several hours, for a chance passer-by to help him. These hours of waiting would often bring bitter tears, for he knew he would be late in reaching home. It was a lonely, dark road, and he was much afraid, and besides, when he did get home, he generally received a severe flogging for being so late.

When Booker was about eight years of age the slaves were liberated, and he, with his mother and brother and sister, set out for West Virginia, where his stepfather worked in the salt mines. The family packed up their few belongings, and, with very little money, set out on the long and tedious journey of several hundred miles. The children walked most of the way, until their feet were sore and blistered. It took them several weeks to make the journey, and they slept, either in the open or in some abandoned cabin by the roadside.

Although he was only a child, Booker was put to work in the salt mines as soon as they reached Maiden, where his stepfather lived. There was no play for him, nothing but hard work. Sometimes he had to rise at four o'clock in the morning, and work until he was nearly dropping from sheer exhaustion.

Once when he was a little fellow, he had taken some books to the school house for his young mistress. He looked in and saw several dozen white boys and girls learning to read and write, and it seemed a wonderful thing to him. He thought that getting into school must be like getting into Paradise. Once he got settled in Maiden a great desire to learn to read came over him. In some way a copy of Webster's spelling book found its way to their cabin, and he eagerly began to learn the alphabet. At that time there was no single person of his race whom he knew, who could spell, and he was afraid to ask the white people. But in some way he learned what the letters stood for, and soon he began to spell out simple words. His mother was totally ignorant, but she encouraged him all she could.

About this time some kind of a school for coloured children was opened in the town, and a young negro who had learned to read was put in charge. Booker's stepfather, however, decided that he could not afford to lose the money that he was earning, and that he must continue to work in the salt mines. This was a most crushing blow to the negro boy who was so anxious to learn. However, he succeeded in persuading the teacher to give him lessons at night, and he worked hard, although he was often tired in body. After a while he was allowed to attend day school, on the understanding that he also did his work in the mines. So he worked in the mines from very early in the morning until nine o'clock, when school opened, and again he returned when school hours were over.

When he did get to school he found difficulties. All the other boys had "store" caps, of which they were very proud. Booker had none, nor had his mother any money wherewith to buy one, but she sewed two pieces of cloth together, which answered for a "cap". The other boys made great fun of his homemade cap, but he knew it was the best that his mother could do, so he tried to ignore their ridicule. Young Booker had heaps of trouble, and difficulties at every turn, but there never was a time in all those hard years when he did not have the determination to secure an education.

One day, while he was working in the mine, young Booker overheard two men talking about an advanced school for coloured boys at some distance away. In the darkness he crept closer, and he heard one of the men say that opportunities for work were provided, so that worthy pupils could pay part of their board, and at the same time be taught some trade. That was a turning point in his life. He determined there and then to get to that school. Once he had formed that resolution, the idea never left him day or night.

By means of very hard work he managed to save enough money to start him on the road to the school, which was known as Hampton Normal and Agricultural Institute. After many hardships and bitter experiences, he arrived there, but when he presented himself before the head teacher she hesitated about taking him in. He was tired after the long, weary journey, and his clothes were worn threadbare. He looked like a worthless tramp. After some hesitation the teacher gave him a broom, and told him to sweep a room.

Did he sweep that room clean? He never tackled anything with so much delight. He swept it, then dusted it four times. He rubbed every piece of furniture in that room until it shone. He felt that his future depended upon the way he cleaned that room. When he had finished the head teacher came and examined his work. She couldn't find a particle of dust anywhere. "I guess you will do to enter this institution," she said.

He spent three years at Hampton. They were hard years in many ways, for he had little money, and besides, he had to learn everything, almost from the beginning. But he was sheer grit, and things which would have discouraged others only made him more determined. He soon gained a grasp of his studies, and, by very hard grinding, worked his way to the front in his classes. After his course was completed he was made a teacher in the institution, and put in charge of a group of Indians, with whom he did remarkably well.

Then a great opportunity opened up for him. A normal school for coloured people was to be opened in Tuskegee, Alabama. A great many schools for coloured children had been opened since the abolition of slavery, but most of the teachers themselves were not educated, and this normal school was instituted for their benefit. Booker T. Washington was asked if he would take charge of it, and he gladly did so. He began his work in a disused shanty with about thirty pupils, practically all of whom had been trying to teach school.

Soon the shanty became too small for those who came, and Booker Washington saw a large, old disused plantation house, which he decided to purchase and use as a school. He succeeded in raising the necessary five hundred dollars, and soon the whole school moved into the larger premises.

Under his leadership the school grew by leaps and bounds. The coloured people were so thankful for the institution that they brought live cattle, as they could afford it, and these animals were used to maintain the institution, and as a means to train the negroes for farming. Very soon the school owned two hundred horses, colts, mules, oxen, calves, and over seven hundred pigs, sheep and goats. It became necessary to add to the buildings, and soon the work of Tuskegee Institute became known the whole world over. After a few years the school which Booker Washington began in an old shanty, had grown to be an institution with eleven hundred pupils and a staff of eighty-six officers and teachers.

Booker T. Washington—now known everywhere as Professor Washington—became one of the greatest orators in the United States. Often he made speeches before tremendous audiences, and always succeeded in raising the white man's idea of the coloured people. He became a close personal friend of Grover Cleveland, at that time President of the United States, and several times he was invited to the White House, to be guest of the President. Later, he visited England, and was welcomed by Queen Victoria, and many of the most distinguished people of Great Britain. He received the honourary degree of Master of Arts from Harvard University, and it is safe to say that the little negro boy, who began life under such great handicaps, became one of the most highly respected of the world's citizens.

CHAPTER VI.
THE IMMIGRANT LAD WHO BECAME A KING OF INDUSTRY.

In November, 1837—the year in which Queen Victoria ascended the throne—Andrew Carnegie was born in Dunfermline, Scotland. His father was a weaver, and before the invention of the steam loom, made a comfortable, if modest, living. Andrew's mother early impressed upon him that economy was a virtue, a lesson which he never forgot in later days. On one occasion Mrs. Carnegie asked her children to repeat a proverb from the Bible. When it came to Andrew's turn, he stood up and said, "Take care of the pence and the pounds will take care of themselves". While Andrew was mistaken in thinking this was in the Bible, it shows how deeply it had been fixed in his mind.

One day Andrew's father came home very dejected. "Andy," he said, "I have no more work." Up till that time all weaving had been done on hand looms, and the introduction of the steam looms threw hundreds of men out of work. Andrew never forgot how bitter and harsh his father's words sounded. "No more work!" That meant no more money, and poverty stared them in the face.

Andrew's father could not obtain work in the town. Hundreds of others, like himself, were thrown out of work. It was no use moving to another town for conditions were the same everywhere. After some anxious days of planning together, the family decided that the only thing to do was to follow the example of some relations and move to the United States.

The Carnegies sold their hand looms and household belongings, and got ready for their long voyage. There were only two children, Andrew and his younger brother, Tom. Those were the days of sailing vessels, and crossing the Atlantic meant a rough voyage of many weary weeks and, after that, long and tiresome railway journeys. Andrew was only eleven at this time.

The family reached Pittsburgh safely and Mr. Carnegie obtained work at a cotton factory. Soon after this Andrew got a position as a bobbin boy, at *one dollar and twenty cents a week*. He was delighted to be actually earning money. At the end of the first week, when his wages were put into his hand, he felt as happy as a king. One dollar and twenty cents, earned by his own efforts; how proud he felt!

The work was hard and the hours of labour very long. He worked from early morning till late at night, with only an interval of forty minutes for dinner. After a time he got another situation which was, if anything, even harder. This work was to fire the boiler and run the steam-engine which drove the machinery of a small factory. The work was so hard that it soon began to tell upon his health. Night and day he was haunted by the possibility of a calamity, and in his sleep he would often put out his hand to test the water-gauge.

Those were dark days for the young Scotch boy, but he determined not to bring his troubles into the home. He was blessed with a keen spirit of determination to succeed and, no matter how hard he found his work, he never complained. There was poverty in the home, but it was honest poverty and he was not ashamed of it. He often had to deny himself pleasures which other boys could afford, and had to wear his clothes long after they had become shabby; but nobody ever heard him grumble or complain.

When he became fourteen Andrew got a position as a telegraph boy at *three dollars a week*. There was not a prouder boy in Pittsburgh. Besides the advance in wages, the work was healthier. He was so overjoyed with his position that soon he began to fear lest he should lose it. He was not acquainted with the business section of the city where he had to deliver most of his messages, but he overcame this by using his excellent memory. He committed to memory the exact location of all the business houses in the principal streets, so that when a telegram was handed to him, he knew at once where it had to be delivered.

His regular habits and attention to his work soon attracted the attention of those over him and at the age of sixteen he was promoted to the position of telegraph operator, at a salary of three hundred dollars a year. This advance came at the right time, for Andrew's father had just died and the burden of carrying on the home fell upon Andrew's shoulders. Soon after this he accepted a position with the Pittsburgh Division of the Pennsylvania Railroad, at an increase of ten dollars a month.

At this time something happened which did much to change his whole life. Through the interest of his superintendent it became possible for him to purchase ten shares in The Adams Express Company for five hundred dollars. Andrew's business instinct led him to see that it was a splendid opportunity, and his mother was just as anxious as he was to make the venture. After a consultation they decided to mortgage their little home and buy the shares. This little transaction was destined to be the forerunner of many successful business deals.

One day, while he was travelling on the railway, a man showed him the model of a sleeping-car. Such things were at that time unknown, but Andrew saw instantly that the invention was a good one, and made arrangements for the inventor to meet the superintendent of the railroad. The outcome was that a company was formed to build sleeping-cars, and Andrew Carnegie was one of the number. Soon after this he was made superintendent of the Pittsburgh division of the Pennsylvania Railroad.

Not long after he was promoted to this position the company began to make experiments with an iron bridge. Up to this time all bridges had been built of wood. The experiments with iron proved successful. There had been so much delay on the railways by the bridges being broken or burned that the cast-iron bridges were welcomed. Mr. Carnegie, with his keen business instinct, saw at once that iron bridges must displace the wooden ones. He formed a syndicate known as The Keystone Bridge Works, and his first undertaking was to build a bridge with a span of three hundred feet over the Ohio River. Thus began the work of iron and steel constructions which Mr. Carnegie followed up until he became known throughout the world as the "Steel King." Before many years had passed Mr. Carnegie not only owned his own immense iron and steel works, but also a fleet of steamers which were used to transport the iron ore across the Great Lakes. He built his own railroad to convey the ore from the lake ports to Pittsburgh, a distance of 425 miles.

In 1900 The Carnegie Steel Company was organized with a capital of one hundred million dollars. The enormous concern gave employment to 45,000 people. One of the plants alone covers an area of seventy-five acres. It is no exaggeration to say that it is by far the greatest manufacturing concern of its kind in the world. When Mr. Carnegie decided to retire he sold out his interest in the steel works for two hundred and fifty million dollars. It was said at that time that he could give away thirty-five thousand dollars a day and never touch his capital. For many years he gave large sums of money for public libraries and other enterprises which seemed to him to be deserving of assistance. Having worked his own way in the world, from a very humble beginning to a position of great power and influence, Mr. Carnegie never had much patience with lazy people. He would never tolerate around him what are known as "dead heads". "Concentration," he said, "is my motto. First, honesty, then industry, then concentration." He expected every one in his employ to be anxious to do their best. Throughout his life he was a man of good habits, and a non-smoker, and attributed his vigor of mind and body to the fact that he avoided anything which would undermine his health. The careful religious training which he received in his humble home in Scotland had a lasting influence for good upon his life. Clean living, honesty, and devotion to his work, no matter how hard it was, made Andrew Carnegie one of the foremost business men of his generation.

CHAPTER VII.
A SHOEMAKER'S APPRENTICE WHO BECAME A GREAT SCHOLAR.

On the last day of November, 1852, a lad was born near the village of Llangernyw, in Denbigshire, Wales. The proud father, who was the village shoemaker, took the baby to church that same day, and there he was baptized—Henry Jones.

Young Henry's parents were poor, and his grandparents were if anything, poorer. His grandfather worked on the estate of the local squire, and as he grew older his wages were repeatedly reduced, until he was receiving only four shillings a week. But even this was not the worst, for he was offered two shillings and sixpence a week. That seemed too much for the old man, and very soon after he died.

The house in which young Henry was born, was very small. It consisted of one small room downstairs, about ten feet square, and another room the same size upstairs. This tiny downstairs room, was almost always terribly overcrowded. It had to serve as kitchen, dining-room, and living-room all in one. Seven persons had their meals each day in that small room. How to find a seat for every one was a problem, but a way out of the difficulty was found by having the children take their meals in relays. Young Henry, being in a great hurry to get out to play, often took his meals standing, or sitting on the doorstep.

When Henry's little baby sister was born, they all wondered how room could be found for the cradle in that already over-crowded room. But there was a way out. The cradle was put upstairs, and a string let down from it through a hole in the ceiling. Whenever the baby cried, the mother bade one of the children pull the string, which rocked the cradle. Many a time Henry's play was interrupted so that he might spend a time pulling that old string.

There was a constant struggle against poverty in that home, for Elias Jones—Henry's father—never earned more than twenty shillings a week, and generally quite a bit less. The food was plain, but wholesome, consisting for the most part of bread and milk and "shot", that is, ground oat-cake and milk. There were no dull moments in that home. It was crowded and restless all day long. Either the mother was cooking or the father was heating his irons in the fire, or some of the children were clamouring for bread and butter, or perhaps a neighbour had dropped in to see if his shoes were ready and then lingered for a chat. In spite of poverty, which sometimes was severe, it was a happy home, for each one sought to help the others.

Henry did not enjoy attending the village school, in fact none of the children in that village did. The schoolmaster was very cruel and ignorant. The cane was very seldom out of his hands. Any fault or error was punished very severely. If a child whispered and the master was not sure which one it was, he thrashed the entire school. In fact, there was wailing and lamentation in that school the whole day long, and small wonder that when four o'clock came each day, the scholars breathed more freely.

When the school holidays came around, each year in June, the boys were sent out in gangs to thin the turnips for the neighbouring farmers. The whole of the five weeks of summer holidays were spent at this work. The boys were paid from eight-pence to one shilling a day, fourpence being deducted if the farmer provided meals. Young Henry Jones went with his brothers to do this hard work when he was only five and a half years old. When evening came he was often too exhausted to walk, and had to be carried home by the bigger boys. From that time until he was taken to work as a shoemaker, Henry helped to thin turnips each year.

While still a very young boy Henry began to help his father make and repair shoes. It was the greatest ambition of his life to become a good shoemaker. One day an incident happened which made him very proud. Toe-caps for boots were just coming into fashion, and they had to be carefully stitched. When it came to putting on the caps, Elias Jones was not sure of himself, so he went over to the school and asked permission for Henry to return home and do the sewing.

When twelve years of age Henry left school to become a shoemaker's apprentice with his father. It was a happy moment in his life when he put on the leather apron. His mother wanted him to be a blacksmith, or a gardener like his brothers, or a grocer, anything in fact, other than a shoemaker, but Henry stubbornly refused to listen. His mind was made up. He wanted to be a shoemaker like his father. The little workshop in which Henry and his father worked, was a little lean-to at the gable-end of the cottage. Out of the window Henry could see a barn and an old thatched cottage. The room was so small that those working had to get into opposite corners so as not to interfere with each other's movements. Sometimes there was a hired workman, and even a fourth place was often made for the local postman, who worked at making and repairing ladies' boots between his arrival with the letters and his departure. Henry used to think that there was so little room for privacy that it was impossible to keep even one's thoughts to oneself.

Henry soon became a good shoemaker. The work was hard, and the hours very long, but he liked it, and there was not a lazy bone in his body. Just at this time something happened which had a great influence over Henry's life. A lad named Tom Redfern, about his own age, came to Llangernyw to take charge of the school; a friendship sprung up between the two, and soon Tom Redfern told Henry of his ambition to attend the university. Soon that same ambition came to Henry, although it seemed madness for him even to think about such a thing, as his parents were so poor, and his own education had been sadly neglected.

For some time Henry was most unhappy. It seemed to him as if there were no way whereby his ambition could be realized. But his purpose became more resolute, and he made up his mind that if at all possible he would reach his goal. At last arrangements were made enabling Henry to attend a school at a place called Pandy, some distance away, three days each week. Henry got out his old schoolbooks and began to attend Pandy School every Monday, Wednesday and Friday. The remaining three days he worked away at his trade harder than ever. There was an examination known as the Queen's Scholarship held each year, and successful students earned the right to attend Bangor Training College for teachers. Henry determined to try for this, although it did seem an almost impossible task. He retired to rest about eight o'clock each evening, and at one o'clock in the morning the village policeman tapped at his window. Then he got up and dressed and worked away at his books until morning came. There was so much to be learned that at times he almost despaired, but he never gave up.

At last the time came for him to try the examination. He went to Bangor in fear and trembling. One of his brothers had loaned him a suit of clothes, and another brother loaned him a watch. He stayed at the college during the days of the examination. There were quite a number of competitors, and only a few could succeed. Henry was appalled by the look of cleverness and by the smart appearance of most of the students. He felt he had made a horrible mistake in even giving in his name. When he was alone he wept like a child and felt he had no chance whatever. Although he was terribly nervous and covered with confusion he did his best, and when the examination results were published, a few weeks later, his name appeared among those who had passed in the first class.

He entered the training college at Bangor and studied hard for two years. He had to be extremely careful, as he had very little money. Throughout those two years he maintained his place at the head of the college list, and then in 1873—when he was just nineteen, he was put in charge of a school at Brynamman, a mining village in Wales. He remained there for two years, greatly beloved by the pupils in the school, and by the people of the village.

Then in 1875 he passed the examinations for entrance into Glasgow University.

The years Henry Jones spent at Glasgow University were packed full of interest for him. There was much hard work for him, and there was a constant struggle with poverty. His parents were not in a position to help him, and sometimes it almost seemed as though he must give up, but somehow a way always opened, and he was able to continue his studies. At the close of his term he sat for an examination, known as the "Clark Fellowship." This was the "blue ribbon," of the University, and, of course, was the most coveted honour among the students. He had no intention of trying for it, but one of the professors, who was interested in him, persuaded him to sit for the examination. He did, and to his amazement, he was awarded the prize, although all the cleverest students of the University, who were eligible, had also tried. In addition to the great distinction the fellowship carried with it a grant of £225 (about $1,100) a year for four years. And then, for the first time in his life, Henry Jones knew what it was to have money to pay his way and a little left over.

A great day came for him, when in 1884 he was elected to a professorship in Bangor College, Wales. He remained there for several years, and then was made a professor in the University of St. Andrews, in Scotland. After three years there—years of hard work, but of great power and wide influence, he was elected to a very important position; that of Professor of Moral Philosophy in Glasgow University. This was one of the great positions in the universities of Great Britain. It was one which only a great scholar could fill and Henry Jones did fill it with credit to himself and with very great profit to the students, for a period of twenty-eight years.

From being a shoemaker's apprentice, Henry Jones rose to a position of great power and influence. It was not by any means an easy road. There was a terrific struggle with poverty, and at times it seemed as though it would be too much for him. But his tremendous perseverence and grit carried him along, and he succeeded to an extent that he had never dared even to dream of. During the Great War he delivered scores of lectures throughout Great Britain and in the United States. His three sons were on the firing line, and the youngest of them was killed in France. Henry Jones died in 1922, and left behind him the memory of a brave and noble life.

CHAPTER VIII.
FROM GIPSY TENT TO PULPIT.

In March, 1860, a family of gipsies camped on a piece of land near Epping Forest, in the south of England. They were shiftless people moving here and there over the country according to their whims. They were not made welcome anywhere, for gipsies have a reputation for dishonesty, and probably this family named Smith were very much the same as other members of their tribe. But one day during their stay in that place—to be exact it was March 31st—a baby boy was born in that gipsy tent, to whom his parents gave the name of Rodney.

Rodney's parents earned their living very much as other gipsies. They travelled up and down the country making and selling baskets, tinware, clothespegs, and recaning cane chairs. Rodney's father—whose name was Cornelius, also made a business of buying and selling horses. Of course, young Rodney grew up without education. He travelled with his parents and soon learned to go from house to house selling clothespegs and other things. He was a bright lad and together with his brothers and sisters, soon knew more about the flowers and birds than most folks. His parents could neither read or write and so he was not burdened with any kind of lessons. He was too young to understand the value of education and so did not worry over that. He was a happy, care-free little fellow, when something happened which changed his whole life.

Rodney's eldest sister was taken ill and the father drove the gipsy wagon to the door of the doctor's house. The doctor climbed the steps of the wagon, leaned over the door and called the sick child to him. "Your daughter has small-pox," he said to Rodney's father. "You must get out of the town at once." The sorrow-stricken man drove his wagon about two miles out of the town to a place called Morton Lane. There he erected a tent and then drove the wagon farther down the lane with the sick child in it. He remained in the wagon with the child while the mother and the other four children lived in the tent. Soon one of the boys was taken ill and he also was removed to the wagon. Those were hard days for Rodney's mother. She would prepare the food for her sick children, then carry it half-way from the tent to the wagon, then give some signal and the father would come for it. In her anxiety the poor mother seemed to approach a little nearer to the wagon each day. One day she came too near. She too, was taken ill, and when the doctor saw her, he said it was smallpox.

For several days the man watched tenderly over his wife and cared for her, but it was of no avail; she gradually sank. Rodney was walking in the lane with his sister Tilly, when his eldest sister called him. "Rodney," she said, "mother's dead." The little gipsy lad fell on his face as though he had been shot. Rodney's mother was only a poor gipsy woman without any education, but she was mother, and the little fellow knew that without her life would be much harder.

After his mother's death Rodney continued to help his father by selling the homemade clothespegs and tinware. He was very proud of the amount of business he could do. Some days he sold nearly nine hundred pegs. He was a bright-eyed little fellow, not at all bashful, and he became a favourite in the towns which the gipsies visited. When women did not wish to buy or seemed to hesitate, he would say: "Come, now, Madam, here you have the best pegs on the market. They will not eat and will not wear clothes out. They will not cry nor wake you up in the middle of the night." If they still hesitated, Rodney would tell them that he had no mother. It was no wonder that with his humour and determination he generally managed to do a good business.

When Rodney was in his early teens his father became a Christian. It made a great change for the better in Cornelius Smith and life in that gipsy wagon became happier. The father was tremendously in earnest. He gave up his habits of drinking, stealing and swearing, and wherever the wagon went he sought some place of worship where he and his family might learn more about God. The change in Cornelius Smith soon impressed the children and Rodney decided to do as his father had done, and committed himself in simple trust to God.

Although he was at this time about fifteen, Rodney Smith could neither read or write. He had never been to school a day in his life. When he opened the Bible to try and read it, he often had it the wrong way up. As he passed along the streets of towns where the wagon was he tried to read the signs over the shops, but it was hard work, and unless they were very simple words he could not make them out. By trying in every spare moment, however, he soon learned to read; slowly at first, but gradually getting on better each day. He bought a dictionary, and it was in constant use. Whenever he came to a word he did not understand, down came the dictionary. He had a good memory, and once he looked up the meaning of a word he seldom forgot it. He read the Bible a great deal and soon he began to hope that some day he might be able to preach. He knew that for ten years he had been roaming about the fields and streets, when he ought to have been at school, but that was not his fault, and he resolved to try and make up for lost time. He was a good singer and he often sang at religious meetings in the towns and villages they visited. Then he became bold enough to deliver short addresses. As he had very little education, and had scarcely read anything, these addresses were very simple, but he was in earnest and did much good.

Just at this time Rev. William Booth—later known as General Booth—began a movement which was known as the Christian Mission. Mr. Booth heard about Rodney Smith, and persuaded him to become a worker with him, and Rodney agreed. This was in 1877, when he was seventeen years of age.

There was tremendous excitement in the gipsy wagon when Rodney stated his intention of becoming a preacher. Rodney strode up and down in front of the wagon with his three or four books under his arm. On the morning of his departure Rodney dressed himself up in the new clothes which he had bought with what little money he had. All his belongings he packed into a box which he had bought for sixty cents. He bade good-bye to his father and his brothers and sisters, and then this young gipsy lad, with very little education and scarcely any money, took the train for London to engage in Christian work. He arrived in London that same evening and went to the people with whom he was to live for the time being. That evening Rodney sat up to a table for a meal, and used a knife and fork, for the first time in his life. He was terribly embarrassed, and when a piece of linen was placed beside his plate he did not know what to do with it. He thought it must be a pocket handkerchief and said so to his hosts. He could see at once that he had made a mistake, and overwhelmed with confusion he said: "Please forgive me, I do not know any better. I am only a gipsy boy, and have never been taught what these things are. I know I shall make lots of blunders, but if you correct me whenever I make a mistake I will be grateful. I will never be angry, and never cross."

A serious difficulty confronted Rodney when he had to conduct his first services alone. He could speak, pray, and sing, but as yet he could read only with difficulty. However, he did his best. He would commence to read a chapter and if he came to big words that he could not pronounce, he would stop and talk a little, then begin to read again at the other side of the big word. He soon became known as a good speaker and an earnest worker. The fact that he was a gipsy attracted people's attention and before long he was speaking regularly to large gatherings.

During the few years following Rodney made great progress. He soon learned to read with ease and his addresses were listened to with great interest. He rose early in the mornings and spent several hours in reading and in devotions. During the afternoons he visited those in need, and in the evenings he addressed meetings both in the open-air and in halls. He was often sent to towns where the work of the Christian Mission was at a very low ebb, but wherever he went it was the same, his earnest preaching and sweet singing attracted the people.

While he was stationed at Hull his congregations were greater than ever. Often fifteen hundred people would be gathered at the Sunday-morning prayer meeting at seven a.m., and the crowds at the regular services were so great that often thousands would be unable to get into the large building. Rodney was by this time married and known as "Gipsy Smith", and the Christian Mission had become the Salvation Army. Under his care the work at Hull grew so that 15,000 copies of the *War Cry* were sold each week.

From Hull Gipsy Smith was sent to Hanley. Here he found a small number of people worshipping in a large building which had been a circus. Soon the old circus which held 2,500 people was crowded to the doors, and crowds as great, if not greater, than those which had gathered at Hull, came to hear the gipsy. There was a great revival of religion and the influence of it was felt for many miles around.

Soon after this Gipsy Smith began work as an evangelist among the churches, and he has continued to do this with great success up to the present time. In 1886, at the earnest request of some friends, he paid his first visit to America. When he arrived in New York he was scarcely known to any and the idea of a gipsy preacher rather startled the ministers and members of the churches. After some hesitation the minister of a large church agreed to have Gipsy Smith conduct a mission in his church. It was a large building, holding fifteen hundred people, but it was packed from the first service, and continued so for the three weeks that the gipsy was there. Soon more requests came in for services than the Gipsy could grant. The newspapers contained glowing accounts of his work, and from all sides came testimonies to the great good that he had done. Thousands of people were blessed under his earnest preaching, and when the time came for him to return to England a vast number of people wished him god-speed.

People who heard Gipsy Smith preach could scarcely believe that he had been born in a gipsy tent and had never spent a day in school. His use of the English language was so good, and his thoughts so fine and clear, that it seemed as if he must have received his training in a university. But he never forgot, himself, nor did he wish any one else to forget, what a very lowly beginning he had.

After his return to England Gipsy Smith became an assistant to the Rev. F. S. Collier, of Manchester. Here he continued to be a means of blessing to great numbers of people. Sometimes he preached to congregations of over five thousand, and always with good results. He soon became known as one of the greatest evangelists of Great Britain and wielded a great influence for good.

Gipsy Smith has paid several visits to America, and each time he has risen higher in the respect and love of the people. Wherever he goes crowds flock to hear him, and they are never disappointed. Americans have learned to look upon his visits as red-letter days for the churches, and if he could be spared from the Homeland, he would be warmly welcomed on this side of the Atlantic.

Gipsy Smith has preached in nearly all parts of the British Empire. He has been, for many years now, one of the great evangelists of the homeland. Thousands of people have been made better by his simple, direct message. Many great men have recognized in him a prophet of God, and they have been glad to honour him as such. He has counted among his friends some of the greatest men living, yet he has never lost his simplicity and gratitude to God for making him what he is. Not long ago he said: "I have had rich and strange experiences. I have lived in many houses, the guest of many sorts and conditions of people. I have been presented to two presidents of the United States, dined with bishops and archbishops. In my study hangs a letter from her late Majesty, Queen Victoria, and another from a royal duchess, but the most treasured things in my home are two pictures which adorn the walls of my bedroom. One is the picture of the wagon in which my mother died, and the other is a picture of a group of gipsies. I never sleep in that room without looking at these pictures and saying to myself: "Rodney, you would have been there to-day but for the grace of God. Glory be to His name for ever."

CHAPTER IX.
A BLIND MAN WHO BECAME POSTMASTER-GENERAL OF ENGLAND.

On August 26th, 1833, just four years before Queen Victoria began to reign, Henry Fawcett was born at Salisbury, England. He was sent to a Dame's school where he did not get on very well. The teacher said that he had a head like a colander, and he was so slow in learning his lessons that he became known as the dunce of the class. Young Harry himself admitted that he did not enjoy school. He loved to be out in the open and in the woods, but he went like a snail, unwillingly, to school.

There was one thing which never failed him and that was his appetite. He was always complaining that he did not get enough to eat. When his family moved away from Salisbury Harry went to a boarding-school, and in nearly every letter he wrote home he said he was nearly starving. In one letter to his mother he said: "Please, when the family has quite finished with the ham bone, send it on to me." However, in spite of his complaints, he grew stronger and bigger every day, until by the time he was ten he was several inches taller than his school mates of his own age.

When he was fourteen he was sent to a school known as Queenwood College and he began to take more interest in his studies. He worked hard while at this school and when he was nineteen he entered the famous Cambridge University. Henry Fawcett was popular with the other students from the first day that he entered Cambridge. He was very tall—over six feet three inches in height—and he moved around the college halls and over the campus with enormous long strides. He had an exceedingly happy and good-natured disposition and was welcome everywhere.

His greatest ambition in life was to fit himself for service as a member of the British Parliament. He desired to enter Parliament for no other reason than that of serving his fellowmen. There were so many laws which seemed to him to be cruel and unjust; so many heavy burdens weighing upon the shoulders of the poorer classes, that he longed with all his heart to be in a position where he could help to make things better.

In order to fit himself for Parliament he began to study law, but he had considerable trouble with his eyes. This was so serious that he was forbidden to do any reading until they were better. He did not complain, but obeyed the physician's orders. He went to stay with his family at Salisbury. It was during this visit that a terrible thing happened. On the morning of September 15, of 1858, he and his father began to climb Harnham Hill, from which a very fine view of the surrounding country could be obtained. Both father and son had their guns, for they hoped to secure some partridge. As they were crossing a field, Henry advanced in front of his father. A partridge arose and the father, who did not see just how near Henry was, fired, and some of the stray shot entered Henry's eyes, and from that moment until his death he was totally blind.

Henry Fawcett was just twenty-five when this terrible accident happened. He was taken back to his father's house in a cart. He remained perfectly calm as he listened to the doctor's verdict. The curtain had fallen and never again could he see the things which other people saw, nor read the books and papers he so dearly loved. But from that day until his death, twenty-six years later, no one ever heard him complain nor give any outward sign of the terrible disappointment which he must have felt. He did not wish people to openly sympathize with him, and the scores of letters which he received from well-meaning people, intended to console him in his misfortune, really gave him pain. He wanted people to forget that he was blind and treat him as one of themselves.

He straightway determined that he would continue to prepare himself to serve the people in Parliament. He knew that he was handicapped, in such manner as perhaps no other statesman had ever been, still he showed a courage and perseverance which was extraordinary.

Soon after his accident he began to walk about in the open. He naturally stumbled at his first step. When some one caught him by the arm to pick him up he said: "Leave me alone; I've got to learn to walk without seeing and I mean to begin at once—only tell me when I am going off the road."

All who knew Henry Fawcett at this time bear witness to his amazing courage and cheerfulness. If he had a heavy heart, he said nothing of it to others. Especially was this true in his relations with his father and mother. Whenever he was with them he was the life of the home, full of mischief as a schoolboy, and with a hearty laugh that made the house ring. "I want to live to be ninety," he said, and he meant it. He was the soul of kindness and good nature. No one ever knew him to say a cruel or unkind thing, or to spread a report that would injure any one. Throughout his life he sought to promote good-will and understanding and he was never happier than when he was helping some one who was in difficulty.

He had a remarkable memory for voices—that is a faculty which often becomes acute in blind people. It was said of him that if he heard a voice once he never forgot it. Sometimes when spoken to by a person whom he had not heard for many years, a puzzled look would cross his face, but it would suddenly clear up as he called the person by name. His sense of hearing became so keen that he could tell when his friends were not feeling as well as usual from their voices. Often he would startle them by saying: "What's the matter with you to-day, you're looking pale?" A man who had not been near him for twenty years once spoke to him and without a moment's hesitation Fawcett called him by name.

Henry Fawcett made two unsuccessful attempts to enter Parliament. He was defeated in Cambridge in 1863 by only eighty-one votes and a few months later he was defeated in Brighton. Many people voted against him because they thought that blindness was too severe a handicap for any man to become really useful in that great assembly. He himself did not think so, however, and he made a third attempt in 1865—when he was thirty-two years of age—and this time he was elected.

It was a proud day for Henry Fawcett when he entered Parliament. After he became blind no one, not even those who loved him most, believed that it was possible. Only a determination that absolutely refused to be thwarted, made his election possible.

Surrounded by many of the greatest statesmen of the nineteenth century, the blind man quietly took his place in Parliament. During his first session there he said very little. He had to learn the ways of Parliament, which is a difficult task for any one, and made much harder in his case. He made his first speech in March, 1866. Unlike most men he had no notes to help him. He had to rely altogether upon his fine memory. His speech was listened to with rapt attention. The picture of this tall, sightless man with earnest voice and manner, cast a spell over the House, and even those who disagreed with him were deeply impressed by his fine appearance and earnest manner.

In the years which followed Henry Fawcett made a great many speeches in Parliament. He was by no means a silent member. In every good cause which came up for discussion his voice was heard, and always on the side of those who needed help. Not only the struggling people of the British Isles interested him, but for several years he fought very hard on behalf of the poor people in far-off India. He became such a champion of the Indians that he was nicknamed, "The member for India," and he received many letters expressing deep gratitude from those people whom he could never hope to see. He entered into a great many political battles, but there was one thing which even his opponents admitted; that was he never sought anything for himself. He laboured hard to help those whose lot he considered was less fortunate than his own.

In 1880 Henry Fawcett was made Postmaster-General of England, a position of very great importance and responsibility. There were over ninety thousand employees under the administration of the postoffice.

One bright spring day Henry Fawcett took up his duties at the General Post Office. He was introduced to the heads of the various departments and to those next in rank. As he began to warmly shake the hands of all to whom he was being introduced, some one whispered to him, "It is not usual for Her Majesty's Postmaster-General to shake hands with any one in the office below the rank of head of a department." It took a good deal to make Henry Fawcett indignant, but that remark pretty nearly did it. He said, "I suppose I am at liberty to make what use I like of my own hands."

He took a very great interest in all who in any way served the Post Office. From the first day that he took over his position he laboured hard to improve working conditions. He interested himself in every employee and nothing ever seemed too much trouble to this blind man of almost infinite patience and sympathy. No doubt his wonderful kindness meant that some took unfair advantage of him, but he found his supreme happiness in realizing that never before in the history of the great English Post-Office system had the work been done so thoroughly and to the satisfaction of the public. One of the great statesmen of that day said that, "The Postoffice could never have a more capable Postmaster-General, nor its officers a truer friend." In December, 1883, he was taken seriously ill with diphtheria, and this was followed by typhoid fever. For a while his life was despaired of, and it illustrates what a large place in the life of his country the blind man had filled, to know that all England read the bulletins which told of his condition. The Queen herself, telegraphed every day, and sometimes oftener. Mr. Fawcett recovered from this illness and was soon at work again as hard as ever. The following year he was honoured with degrees from many great universities, including Oxford and Glasgow. Then in November, 1884, he was taken suddenly ill and quietly passed away in the presence of his wife and daughter and several friends. He who had lived in total darkness for nearly thirty years; years in which he was never once heard to murmur or complain, passed into the eternal light of God's presence.

A whole nation mourned deeply when this man of such magnificent courage was laid to rest in the quiet churchyard at Salisbury, where he had been born. Tributes to his memory were paid to him by the greatest in the land. Queen Victoria wrote a most touching letter to his widow, and Hon. W. E. Gladstone said that no man had become more deeply enshrined in the memory of his fellow-countrymen. The terrible handicap of blindness had not prevented Henry Fawcett from becoming one of the greatest men of his generation.

CHAPTER X.
THE PLOUGHBOY WHO BECAME A FAMOUS NATURALIST.

One evening, in the town of Dunbar, Scotland, an excited lad hurried through the streets shouting to his schoolmates: "I'm gaun tae Amaraka the morn!" When they refused to believe him he said, "Weel—just you see if I am at skule the morn."

The lad was John Muir. That evening, as he and his brother, David sat by the fireside learning their lessons, his father walked in and said, "Bairns, you needna learn your lessons the nicht, for we're gaun to America the morn!" The boys were wild with joy. Even the natural heart-pain of parting from their grandparents, whom they deeply loved, was quickly quenched as they conjured up pictures of the life they were to lead across the seas. Mr. Muir decided to take with him John, who was eleven years of age, David, a brother, aged nine, Sarah, who was thirteen. Mrs. Muir and four children remained in Scotland until the new home was ready for them.

After a voyage of nearly seven weeks, in a sailing ship, the immigrants arrived in America and very soon after settled on their claim in Wisconsin. With the help of some neighbours, Mr. Muir built a shanty in less than a day, after the materials for the roof and walls were ready. From the first John Muir fell in love with his surroundings. To him the wilderness was a glorious place. He watched the birds and animals, the trees and the flowers, the streams and lakes—everything around him filled him with delight. It was a backwoods farm, and the hard work of clearing the farm began at once. John enjoyed piling up immense quantities of brushwood and making huge fires. Mr. Muir bought a yoke of oxen and the task of clearing the land began in earnest. The lads were up early and late, doing their best to help their father get the place cleared and a frame house built, so that the other members of the family, who had been left behind in Scotland, could join them. Late in the fall, just before the winter snow began to fall, the house was ready, and Mrs. Muir and the other four children arrived.

John was the eldest of the boys, and his father looked to him to do almost a man's work. The summer work was heavy, and especially harvesting and corn-hoeing. All the ground had to be hoed over the first few years and John had scarcely a minute to rest. They had no proper farm implements to begin with, and the hoes had to be kept moving up and down as if they were worked by machinery. John took great pride in the amount of work he was able to do, and very often worked sixteen and seventeen hours a day.

In winter time John and his brothers arose early to feed the cattle, grind axes, bring in the wood, and dozens of other jobs that needed to be done. No matter what the weather was, there was work to be done. It was pioneer farming, and it was only by long and hard effort that it was possible to earn a livelihood.

John was put to work at the plough at twelve years of age, when his head little more than reached the handles. For many years the bulk of the ploughing on that hard backwoods farm fell to his lot. From the first he determined to do as good ploughing as though he were a man, and in this he did not fail. None could draw a straighter furrow. The work was made especially hard because of the tree stumps which were everywhere on the half-cleared land.

To John's lot also fell the task of splitting rails for the long lines of zig-zag fences. Making rails was hard work and required no little skill. Sometimes John would cut and split one hundred rails a day from short, knotty, oak timbers, swinging the heavy mallet from early morning to late at night, until his hands were sore. He was proud of the amount of work that he was able to do, but the heavy exertions of those days probably prevented his growth and earned for him the title of the "Runt of the Family."

After eight years of very hard work the farm was at last cleared. John had worked as hard as any man, often rising at four o'clock in the morning and toiling till late at night. He made the rash vow that he would do a man's work, and even when he was not well, he made good his pledge. Then, when at last the land was cleared, his father bought a half section of wild land four or five miles away, and the task of clearing, breaking up, and fencing began all over again.

Soon after the entire family moved to the new farm, which was known as Hickory Hill Farm. It was high and dry, and very good land, but there was no living water, and so a well, ninety feet deep, had to be dug. With the exception of the first ten feet of ground, was hard, fine-grained sandstone. Mr. Muir tried to blast the sandstone, but failed, and he decided to have John do all the work with mason's chisels. This was a long, hard job, with a good deal of danger in it. He had to sit cramped in a place about three feet in diameter, and chip, chip away, day after day, for months. In the morning Mr. Muir and David lowered John in a windlass, then went away to the farm work and returned at noon to haul him up for dinner. After dinner he was promptly lowered again and left there until evening.

One day he was almost suffocated by carbonic acid gas which had settled at the bottom during the night. He was almost overcome as soon as he had been let down, but managed to shout, "Take me out". He was hauled up almost more dead than alive. Water was thrown down to absorb the gas, and a bundle of hay attached to a light rope was dropped and used to carry down pure air to stir up the poison. At last water was secured and two iron-bound buckets swung, which drew water from the well for many a long year.

It was fortunate for John that he had made good progress at school before he left Scotland, for he had few opportunities to study after he arrived on the backwoods farm.

For many years nearly every waking moment was spent in doing some kind of manual work. However, he was hungry for knowledge, and eagerly read the few books which came his way. Among these were the Bible, parts of Shakespeare's poems, and selections from Milton, Cowper and others, not often read by boys of his age.

When he was twenty-three he decided to attend the State University. His father told him that he would have to support himself by his own efforts. This he did, first by living very simply, and then by seizing every opportunity to earn a dollar. He taught school and worked in the harvest fields during the long summer vacations. When in college he lived so frugally that sometimes he did not spend more than half a dollar a week.

The greatest interest of John Muir's life had always been the things he found in nature. From the days when, as a little fellow, he played around the fields and streams near Dunbar in Scotland, he had loved the open air and the hundreds of things which lived and grew there. When he did finish his course at college he suffered from eye trouble, and was even threatened with blindness. He there and then decided to live in the open and see as much of the world as possible.

He set out on a walking tour through several States. He visited Cuba, then the Isthmus of Panama, and then went straight to San Francisco, where he arrived with less than a dollar in his pocket. This distance was all covered on foot. He slept in the open most of the time and gathered biological specimens as he went. Sometimes he ran completely out of money, and when this happened he secured work until he had sufficient to proceed.

Soon after he arrived in San Francisco he visited the Sierra Nevada Mountains, and from then until the time of his death he found these great hills a source of never-ending joy. He tramped among them until he knew them thoroughly. It was chiefly through his efforts that Congress set aside Yosemite as a national park. He was often called "Father of the Yosemite."

In 1876 he was appointed a member of the United States Coast and Geodetic Survey, and he saw Alaska, where he travelled hundreds of miles alone. Later he visited Siberia, Norway, and Switzerland. He did not hurry through those lands as many tourists do, but wherever he went he studied, with much care, the flowers and the animals that lived in the great open spaces. Things which others passed with only a glance he closely observed. His passion to study these things led him to visit India, Russia, Australia, New Zealand, Brazil and many other countries. He travelled thousands of miles on foot and generally slept in camps and tents.

He wrote several books and a great many articles which appeared in the big magazines. He wrote about animals, insects, and flowers, and his information was gained at first hand. He knew these things because he lived among them and loved them. His knowledge was recognized and appreciated. Harvard and several other universities conferred honourary degrees upon him, but he cared little for these things. From his travels abroad he returned to the Sierra Mountains which he loved so passionately. Several universities invited him to become professor, but he preferred to live his simple life among the mountains. After his death, in 1914, these beautiful lines were written about him by Odell Shepard:

THE PRAYER OF JOHN MUIR.

Let me sleep among the shadows of the mountain when I die,
  In the murmur of the pines and gliding streams,
    Where the long day loiters by
    Like a cloud across the sky,
  And the night is calm and musical with dreams.

Lay me down within a canyon of the mountains, far away,
  In a valley filled with dim and rosy light;
    Let me hear the streams at play
    Through the vivid golden day,
  And a voice of many waters in the night.

Let me lie where glinting rivers ramble down the slanting glade,
  Under bending alders, garrulous and cool,
    Where the sycamores have made
    Leafy shrines of shifting shade,
  Tremulous about the ferned and pebbled pool.

CHAPTER XI.
A SICK MAN WHO NEVER GAVE UP.

Francis Parkman was born at Boston on September 16, 1823. He had a fairly good start in life. He lived in a fine large brick house of three stories, with good big lawns and lots of room, so that any boy could have a real good time. There were flowers and fruit trees in abundance, and no doubt young Francis thought himself a very lucky boy.

When he was eight years of age he went to live on a farm with his grandfather, and remained there for nearly five years. It was during this time that he began to take a keen interest in nature. When not at school he spent most of his time collecting eggs, insects, reptiles, trapping squirrels, woodchucks, and other animals. All his life he was greatly interested in animals, and many good stories are told about him. Once when he was sitting at his desk in school a snake which had revived in the warmth of the schoolroom stuck its head out of his pocket, much to the consternation and alarm of some pupils sitting near.

His father was a minister, and one Sunday morning while Rev. Dr. Parkman and his wife were walking solemnly down the street to church with Francis close behind, Mrs. Parkman noticed a smile on the faces of those they passed. She turned around to see what was the matter, and there was Francis carrying by the tail, at arm's length, a dead rat. His father made him throw away the rat and walk with more dignity.

His favourite subject at school was history. He was especially interested in reading about Indians. By the time he was seventeen he made up his mind to write a history of the Indian wars, and this resolution became the controlling power of his life. From that time on he never lost an opportunity of studying Indian life. Nearly all his vacations were spent either with Indian tribes or in carefully going over ground which had been the scenes of many fierce conflicts.

About this time Francis Parkman began to have trouble both with his eyes and his heart. He consulted several doctors and travelled extensively, seeking to improve his health. For this reason, and also in order to better acquaint himself with the manners and customs of Indians, he joined a band of Indians on their way to the remote West. During this extensive trip he suffered great pain, yet he knew that it would be unwise to complain or show signs of weakness. Day after day he faced the hardships of a strange life, riding daily on horseback over a wild country, and taking his share with the Indians in hunting buffalo.

Instead of improving his health this trip greatly weakened him, and probably did him permanent injury. He could not digest the food that was given him; he became so faint and dizzy that he had to be helped into the saddle, and at times his mind lost its clearness. He could not sleep at nights, and from that time until his death he rarely, if ever, enjoyed a good night's sleep. When he got three hours' sleep out of twenty-four he thought himself lucky. Most of the time he got even less than this. He was attacked with rheumatic gout, which particularly affected one of his knees. This caused him intense suffering, and for many years he could only hobble around with the aid of a stick.

Francis Parkman, while still in his early twenties, was a sick man. He had so many disorders that he was never free from pain. Often the pain was so intense that he could not concentrate on any subject. He used to refer to his many troubles as "the enemy", and this can be said to his credit, that he never ceased to fight "the enemy". He had amazing courage; probably not one man in ten thousand could have been so brave and cheerful with so much physical pain.

He felt his misfortunes all the more because he so much admired strong men. As a boy, one of the great ambitions of his life had been to become strong physically. One thing which he so much admired about the Indians was their great agility and endurance. And so very early in life, he began to avoid habits which would undermine his strength. For such a man, admiring the physically strong as he did, it became a terrible trial for him to have to go through life as an invalid.

In the spring of 1848 he began to write the "History of the Conspiracy of Pontiac." He did this partly because he felt that to have a strong purpose, and to keep his mind occupied, would help him partly to forget his troubles. In view of his condition it was a great task to attempt. His eyes were so extremely weak that he could not write his own name except by closing them. His brain would not permit him to work for more than a few minutes at a time. Every effort he made cost him a good deal of pain. He caused a wooden frame to be constructed of the same size and shape as a sheet of paper. Stout wires were fixed horizontally across it, half an inch apart, and a movable back of thick pasteboard fitted behind them. The paper for writing was placed between the pasteboard and the wires, guided by which, and using a black lead crayon, he could write fairly well with closed eyes.

He made notes for his book with eyes closed, and these were afterwards read to him until they had become thoroughly fixed in his memory. But under such terrible handicaps did he work, that for a year and a half he only averaged six lines of writing each day.

The fact that he could not use his eyes in writing made his work very slow indeed. He had to depend upon the eyes of others. Often he would go to a public library with some educated person and for hours listen to passages from books which were likely to help him. If he had been well he could have seen at a glance what books were worth spending his time over. As it was he had to listen to a great many unimportant and tedious details.

Even when he was fairly well his condition was such that he could not listen to any person reading for more than an hour or two each day and that with frequent intervals of rest. It was all painfully slow and tedious work and it is not hard to believe what he wrote in the following words: "Taking the last forty years as a whole, the capacity for literary work which during that time has fallen to my share has, I am confident, been considerably less than a fourth part of what it would have been under normal conditions."

In 1851 Francis Parkman published "The Conspiracy of Pontiac" in two volumes. Fourteen years later he published "The Pioneers of France in the New World". Then followed, "The Jesuits in North America", "LaSalle and the Discovery of the Great West", "The Old Regime", "Count Frontenac and New France under Louis XIV", "Montcalm and Wolfe" and "A Half Century of Conflict".

All those books were marked by the author's extraordinary accuracy. One could have forgiven a man who was in such great pain if he had shown signs of carelessness, yet a lack of thoroughness was the one thing which annoyed Francis Parkman. He expected other people to be thorough and painstaking in their work, and he carried it out in his own life. If there was the least doubt about any statement he would not rest until he had looked carefully into the matter. As a result his books probably rank as the most reliable authorities on Indian life, customs and history. The thoroughness and accuracy of his books is admitted by all. During the period 1848 to 1867 he never knew a day when his body was not racked with pain, and yet the books he wrote during these years of severe suffering are a model of first-class workmanship.

Many great universities hastened to honour the scholar who had worked under such great difficulties. In 1879 McGill University conferred on him the degree of Doctor of Laws and Languages, and Harvard University honoured him with the same degree in 1889. He was made an honourary member of over twenty scientific societies in Great Britain and America. He died in 1893 at the age of seventy. Thus came to an end the life of one who, in spite of terrible handicaps, became one of the greatest historians of his age.

CHAPTER XII.
HOW A POOR BOY BECAME A GREAT SCIENTIST.

Just a few days before Christmas, in 1823, a little boy was born in the French village of Saint Leons. His parents were very poor, and the young boy, whose name was Jean Henri Fabre, was sent to live with his grandparents, who tilled a small farm some miles away. There he lived until he was seven, and made friends with the calves, the sheep, the geese and the hens, who were almost his sole companions.

His grandparents had no education. They had never opened a book in their lives. They had lived all their lives in that lonely farmhouse, and they knew little, and cared less, about the outside world. The grandfather was a stern old man, with his serious face, and unclipped hair, which he generally brought behind his ears with a flick of his thumb. He wore curious breeches, buckled at the knees, and heavy wooden shoes stuffed with straw. Young Henri was devoted to his old grandmother, who, while she could not read, told the little fellow many a thrilling story.

When meal time came all the members of the family, big and little, sat round the table, which consisted of long planks laid over two benches. At one end of the table would be a huge loaf of rye bread, which only the grandfather was allowed to cut. The grandmother generally attended to the bacon and turnips, which formed the staple food. Sometimes, on special occasions, there would be a good supply of homemade cheese. There were no proper beds in the little home, but as Henri was the youngest, he was given a sack, stuffed with oat-chaff, upon which to sleep.

In spite of the poverty of his surroundings, Henri was not unhappy. He was too young to worry much about his appearance. It is true that his clothes were rough and shabby. He generally wore a rough frieze frock which flapped against his bare legs, but his hardships were forgotten in his great love for the animals around that little farm. He loved the flowers, but even more he loved the living things all around him. Butterflies, grasshoppers, bees, spiders, wasps, in fact, every living thing the boy watched, and, when in the evening the family sat around the rough table to eat, Henri told them of his love for all these creatures. The other members of the family just laughed at Henri. How little they thought that some day Henri would know more about these insects than any one else in the world. When he was seven the time came for him to go to school, so he returned to his father's house in Saint Leons. The school he attended, which was the schoolmaster's home, consisted of one room, which had to serve as school, kitchen, bedroom, dining-room, and, sometimes, chicken-house and piggery. The schoolmaster himself was not a man of much learning, and seemed more interested in his chickens and pigs than in anything else, but he managed to teach the pupils their letters and some elementary subjects. Often in the middle of a lesson the door would be burst open, and a dozen hungry little pigs would scamper in, followed by a brood of chickens. By the time they had been put out the schoolmaster would have considerable difficulty in getting his scholars' attention back to the lesson. It was a noisy school indeed. All the boys loved the arithmetic lesson because it gave them a chance to shout. The whole class would recite the multiplication table in unison, and they would simply yell until even the little pigs became scared, and bolted out of the school.

Just about this time something happened which had a great influence over Henri Fabre. As a reward for doing well at school he was given a prize—a book about animals, with scores of pictures in it. True, it was only a cheap edition, with paper covers, but to Henri it seemed priceless. How he pored over its contents, and looked at the pictures of coons, foxes, wolves, dogs, cats, asses, rabbits, and dozens of other animals! This served to kindle his love for living things, and when the schoolmaster told the boys to go into his garden and kill the insects Henri crammed them into his pockets. Snails, beetles, and even wasps, all seemed to him too interesting to be ruthlessly killed.

When Henri was ten his parents moved from Saint Leons to the town of Rodez. There he attended a school where he was granted free tuition for rendering certain services in the chapel. Attired in a surplice, red skull-cap, and cassock, he, together with three other boys, performed his services in the chapel, and received instruction of a much more advanced character than he had yet received. Some of the studies he found difficult, and if he had listened to the call of the woods, he would often have played truant, for he was much more interested in the living things he found there than in the dry subjects learned in the school. But he remembered his poor parents at home, and their anxiety to see him make progress, so he stuck to even the most difficult tasks, and his record there was a good one.

Soon after this misfortune visited his family, and Henri had to leave school, and for some considerable time he suffered many hardships. He often went without food, and wandered along the highroads, selling lemons at country fairs, and later working at the building of a railway. Just at that time he was fortunate in winning a bursary for the normal school at Avignon, and so ended a period of his life which had been exceedingly dark.

During the years he spent at Avignon he pursued his studies with earnest purpose, and acquitted himself with distinction. He gained his college diploma, and was appointed to teach in a school at Carpentras, and after some years of close study he was made Professor of Physics and Chemistry at Ajaccio.

During these years Henri Fabre's interest in insects had been steadily increasing. Little creatures that other people thought ugly, he studied and loved. One day a naturalist, who had been attracted to Fabre, was explaining some things to him of unusual interest. Suddenly the naturalist took a pair of scissors and burst open a shell, and then explained to Fabre the anatomy of a snail. That incident opened a new world for Fabre. His interest in insects, which had always been great, became extraordinary. No longer was he content to study the outward form of insects, but he dissected and thoroughly examined all that came within his range. Often late at night, or again early in the morning, when other people were in their beds, he searched the country lanes and pools for specimens of insects, and then studied them closely to find out their habits of life.

Soon Henri Fabre became recognized as one who understood insect life as well, if not better, than any other living person. This is not to be wondered at, for an insect, which to other people, meant nothing, was a subject of great interest to him. If he were walking along the highway and an insect appeared, he would leave another man to follow it and study its movements, and he was quite indifferent as to what people thought of him. One day, when in his home, an unusually interesting wasp appeared; he dropped what he was doing and watched its movements for hours, utterly forgetting everything else.

Although so well known and respected as a great scientist, Henri Fabre was still poor. His income did not amount to much more than three hundred dollars a year. Then he was made a member of the Legion of Honour, one of the greatest distinctions which could be awarded to any man. He was introduced to the Emperor of France, and soon the French people everywhere began to look upon him with great pride. In spite of his great fame, he was a comparatively poor man, but his habits of life were simple, and he did not long for fame. He was supremely happy when left alone to study the tiny creatures of the insect world.

In 1879, Fabre retired from the college at Avignon to Serignan. There, more than ever, he had time to follow the bent of his life, and then he began to publish his famous books about insects, which are so fascinating. One after another, his books were printed, and all over the world people began to look upon these books as works of authority. He wrote: "The Life of the Spider", "The Life of the Fly", "The Life of the Caterpillar", "The

Life of the Grasshopper", "The Life of the Weevil", "The Glow-worm and other Beetles", and a great many other books upon subjects of which very few people knew much.

The methods of his research were very simple—a magnifying-glass, two scalpels, made by himself from needles, a saucer for his dissecting trough, empty match-boxes and sardine tins for his specimen cases, a few wires under which he could imprison insects and watch them—these were about the only things he needed. He had extraordinary patience, and he loved with great tenderness the creatures whose habits he studied.

Fabre lived to be ninety-two years of age. He died in 1915, while the Great War was raging. Before his death his real genius was recognized all over the world. The foremost scientific societies of England, Sweden, Belgium, Russia and other lands hastened to confer honourary titles upon him, and while he himself was so simple and modest that he cared little for fame, the honours conferred showed how highly he was esteemed. From being a very poor boy, Henri Fabre became one of the greatest scientists that ever lived.

CHAPTER XIII.
WHAT AN ILLITERATE BOY MADE OF HIS LIFE.

Just seven days before Christmas, 1851, a baby was born at Mansfield, Nottingham, England, named James Flanaghan, who was destined to have a pretty hard time of it for several years. The baby's father was Patrick Flanaghan, and, as his name would suggest, was Irish by nationality. When he was sober, Patrick Flanaghan was a good husband and father, but when he was drunk—which was pretty often—he acted like a beast. At the sound of his unsteady step on the stairs, his wife and children prepared for the worst. Often what little furniture there was in the Flanaghan home would be smashed to atoms in the fury of the man's drunken passion, and the mother and children would be driven out into the street, to wander around until some one had pity on them and took them in.

After a few years James went to work with his father at the task of pipe-making in a factory. His father was the kiln man, and was clever in the art of giving fixity to moulds of clay by a process of burning. James stood at the table modelling clay into tobacco pipes. It was hard work for the boy, and all he received was sixty cents a week. The father became dissatisfied with such small wages, and so James was taken out of the factory to work in a coal mine.

A lady, in whose class James sat at Sunday school, gave him a coat which was several sizes too large for him. His mother wept when she saw him; he looked so funny; but James was too young to worry over his appearance, and he was glad to have a coat to keep him warm.

The men with whom James worked down the mine, teased him or cursed him, according to their moods. They were rough men and often their language was vile. At meal times James munched his crust of bread and cheese, and heard tales which had been told in the saloon the night before.

Soon he was taken, along with other lads of his age, to the saloon. His sweet singing astonished and pleased the drunken men there. He sang songs which he had heard, and he attended theatres, and such was his memory that he could reproduce whole scenes that he had witnessed. For all this James received a good deal of praise, and especially from the saloon-keepers, who were glad to have any one who could attract men to their drinking places.

Through the influence of a Sunday-school worker, named Parker, James was induced to attend a religious service at a Methodist church. He sat very reverently through the service although it all seemed very strange to him, and much of it he did not understand. When at the close of the service a man took him by the hand and said: "God bless you, my brother," he was deeply touched, and his eyes filled up with tears. He was not accustomed to that kind of speech. It was the kindness of the people which led him back to that church again. Deep impressions for good were made on the young lad's mind, although he could not make up his mind what to do. He had a great many evil companions, and he knew it would be a difficult thing for him to break away from them; however, one Sunday morning as he sat in church, listening to an earnest sermon, he bowed his head, and gave himself to God. It was the turning-point in James Flanaghan's life.

He was at this time about sixteen years of age, but he had practically no education. He could not write his own name, nor even distinguish the letters of the alphabet. He had never been to school one day in his life, and practically all he knew was the vulgar sayings he had heard in the mine, and in the saloons. But he began to improve himself at once, and, big fellow though he was, he bought an alphabet and learned his letters thoroughly, and then he began the simplest kind of reading. Often when he came home from the mine, tired though he was, he sat up until past midnight trying to make up for lost years.

He tried hard and made good progress. As soon as he was able to read well enough to spell out the words, he committed to memory the One Hundred and Third Psalm. It took him quite a while to learn it all for he could only commit to memory a few verses at a time, but he succeeded, and this fine psalm filled his mind with beautiful thoughts during the hours he spent down the mine. Then soon afterwards when there was need for teachers in the Sunday School he offered his services. He was given the beginners' class at first, for he could neither read nor teach the lessons for older scholars, but as he advanced in knowledge he was promoted to other classes, and after a few years was actually made superintendent of the school.

There was a group of earnest men in that church, who, like Flanaghan, worked hard, but who on Sundays preached either in small churches and mission halls of the district, or in the open air. Soon he joined them, and although his first prayers and brief addresses in public were halting and a source of anxiety to him, he rapidly improved, and all the neighbouring churches were glad to have him preach in their pulpits. Miners who had known him for several years could not understand how he had become educated so quickly. They knew that he had never been a day at public school in his life and that even at sixteen he could neither read nor write. Yet now he could read whole chapters of the Bible in public, and could preach sermons that showed he had read many other books as well. He was still working fourteen hours a day in the mine, and his time for reading was strictly limited, but he never wasted a moment, and his perseverance and earnestness, together with his excellent memory, soon enabled him to preach as though he had attended school as other young men.

Soon after this he was asked to conduct some services at a village named Long Clawson. These services were so successful that he was engaged to conduct further services in that district for a period of six months. Of course, this meant giving up work in the coal mine, and moving elsewhere. The news quickly spread throughout the little town where he lived, and the people came to his house to wish him and his wife and children "God speed." His conversion, and the marvellous progress he had made in education were widely known, and all were deeply interested. He stood upon a chair, and the crowd gathered around. He told them again of his conversion, and after a few earnest words, bade them a tender farewell. All were deeply moved and there were few dry eyes.

For four years James Flanaghan did the work of an evangelist; making visits, varying from ten days to four weeks, at many places throughout the country. Whenever he could spare half an hour he spent it in reading. He knew that he had a great deal of ground to make up, and he never could make it up unless he worked hard. His careful reading soon showed in his sermons and addresses. Not only were his public speeches earnest, they were thoughtful, and people who had known him in other years considered his progress nothing short of a miracle.

Then he was appointed city missionary for the city of Nottingham. During the time he lived there James Flanaghan became widely known and greatly beloved. The services he conducted at the large mission hall were the most important gatherings he had ever addressed. The large building held two thousand people and quite often it was filled to overflowing. A brotherhood organization for men was established with over two thousand members, and the entire city of Nottingham was influenced for good. When the time came for him to leave the city, he carried away with him the good wishes of all.

In 1891, when he was forty years of age, James Flanaghan was made a minister of the Primitive Methodist Church. This was a somewhat unusual thing to do, as he had never been to college, nor taken any regular course of study, but his work had shown that he was a true and able servant of God and he would never disgrace the ministry, for his close study for more than twenty years had made him a well-educated man.

His first charge after ordination was at Trinity Street Church, London. Here he found a large church, almost empty, yet surrounded by a vast population of very poor people. His first Sunday was not an encouraging one. There were only thirty-six people at the morning service, and thirty-seven in the evening, but James Flanaghan had been facing difficulties all his life, and had become used to them. From the time when, as a baby he had been turned out into the streets with his poor mother, up to the time he stood in the big empty church at London, it had been a bitter, uphill struggle, but rough weather makes good sailors, and Flanaghan's heart was strong and brave.

The more he learned about the district around his church the more he realized the need for Christian work. There were scores of low-class drinking places, and the lodging-houses were little better than haunts for animals. There was one lodging house where thirteen murders had been committed, but the very wretchedness of the district made an appeal to Flanaghan's sympathy, and he worked harder than he had ever worked in his life; if that were possible. Soon the large building was filled. Fine, enthusiastic meetings were held during the week and hundreds of boys in that neighbourhood enjoyed their first games in the gymnasium of the church.

Soon the premises, which had seemed so large and empty at first, were far too small to hold all the people who were eager to attend. What was to be done? The people of the district certainly could not raise money to enlarge the premises, and so it was decided that Mr. Flanaghan should visit towns and cities outside of London during the week, and by lecturing and preaching raise sufficient money to build larger and better premises. In less than two years Mr. Flanaghan had raised the sum of twenty thousand dollars, which made it possible to begin work on the new buildings.

By this time the name of James Flanaghan had become known throughout England. Just the announcement on a billboard that "James Flanaghan is coming," was a sufficient advertisement to fill any church or hall. Under the magic spell of his eloquence people became generous in their gifts for the poor. Poor children brought their coppers to buy a new brick in the buildings. A man who was penniless put his watch and chain on the collection plate, while another man brought a hen and requested that it be sold, and the funds used as the speaker wished.

The new hall was formally opened on January 4th, 1900, and is known as St. George's Hall. It is a fine, well-equipped building, and from the day it was opened until the present time it has been a means of blessing to thousands of people in that crowded section of London, known as Bermondsey, where people live under conditions which, fortunately, are almost unknown in this land.

James Flanaghan's reputation spread overseas, and in 1908 he was invited to tour Australia and New Zealand. He received a great welcome in New Zealand by people of all denominations. Arrangements had been made for large meetings, but in most cases the churches and halls which had been engaged were much too small. No visitor to that land for many years so favourably impressed the people. Audiences were held spellbound by his eloquence. How few of those who so admired his culture and lofty thought realized that they were listening to a man who had never been to public school a day in his life, and who up to the time of his sixteenth birthday could neither read or write. Lord Plunkett, the Governor of New Zealand, greatly admired Mr. Flanaghan, and showed him much kindness. Sir J. C. Ward, the Prime Minister, made him an honoured guest of the Parliament, and wherever he went his fine bearing and culture made an excellent impression. When he left he received the thanks of all the Christian Churches. A similar welcome was extended to him in Australia, and there he was for some time the guest of Lord Chief Justice and Lady Way.

He returned to his work in England, and found time to write several books, which had a wide circulation and did much good. Such were the demands for his services that only a small percentage of the requests could be acceded to, but he led a busy life and exerted much influence for good.

In 1914 he was taken ill, and a year later he had to retire from active work. This was a great trial to one who so loved his work, but he gradually became weaker. He died on March 30th, 1918, and his passing was regretted by thousands throughout the world. Members of the British Parliament, mayors, aldermen and councillors of London and the provinces joined the bereaved family in the church and placed flowers upon his grave. All were glad to honour the memory of one who, though he had started life under heavy handicaps, had made his life one of blessing and usefulness to a vast number of people.

CHAPTER XIV.
A DONKEY BOY WHO BECAME A FAMOUS SCULPTOR.

A few miles from the city of Sheffield in England there is a little village named Norton. It was on a tiny farm, near this village, that Francis Chantrey was born on April 7th, 1781. He learned the alphabet at home, and then at the age of six he went to the village school. The old school register is still in existence. It shows that he began to read in April 1787; to write in January, 1788; and to learn arithmetic in October, 1792. The register also shows that Francis often missed school; often for weeks and months at a time. Children were not compelled to attend school in those days, and as his parents were poor, it seems likely that Francis worked around the farm, driving cattle and working hard in the fields.

In those days the city of Sheffield was supplied with milk from the outlying farms. The milk was put into barrels, and two barrels were slung across a donkey's back, one to balance the other. The barrels had taps and the milk was drawn off into tins for house-to-house delivery. Many of the small boys, who drove the donkeys, became notorious for mischief. Often a donkey would refuse to budge an inch, and then the young driver would apply the whip with all his might, while the ass would fix its forelegs into the ground and throw up its hind legs in an effort to dislodge the driver. Very often there would be so much jumping around that the milk must have been nearly churned into butter.

One morning Francis Chantrey was sauntering along with his donkey when he came across a cat sitting on a wall. He made friends with pussy, and seeing a hollow place in the wall, he poured in some milk, and watched the cat drink. Next morning when he came to the same place the cat was there waiting for her breakfast, and he was so pleased that he gave her another supply. That continued for a long time. Each morning—no matter what the weather was—pussy was at her place by the hollow in the wall, and Francis never failed to pet her and leave a supply of milk.

He called his donkey "Jock", and one day when he had delivered all his milk in the city, he was returning with the week's supply of groceries, when Jock stopped to drink at a pool by the side of the road. The donkey found the water so cool and refreshing that before Francis Chantrey had time to prevent him, he slid down into the water, groceries and all. He was just about to roll over and over, when his young master made him get up. As it was, all the tea, sugar and other groceries were soaked, and it was a cross boy who tried to recover what he could from the pond with a rake.

Sometimes when Francis walked by the side of Jock to and from Sheffield, he would amuse himself by whittling a stick with his pocket-knife. One day he was doing this when a gentleman met him, and examined his work, and then asked what it was. "It is the head of Old Fox," said Francis, whose schoolmaster was named Fox. The man thought the carving was so good that he gave Francis sixpence, and that was the first money he ever earned by his carving.

The boy loved drawing pictures, and as the floor of his humble home was of stones, or flags as they are called in English farmhouses, he used to draw pictures upon the floor each Saturday before his mother scrubbed the floor. No doubt his mother often thought the drawings were so good that it was a shame to wash them off.

One day a gentleman came to Mr. Chantrey to do some business, and Mrs. Chantrey brought out a large pork pie, upon the top of which were worked cleverly in paste, a sow and several pigs. When the man saw it, he exclaimed: "What a shame that you should have gone to the expense of getting such a pie for me." When Mrs. Chantrey explained that she had made the pie herself, and Francis had modelled the young pigs, when the dough was soft, he was amazed at the boy's ingenuity.

Francis' father died when he was twelve years of age, and soon after he was apprenticed to a Mr. Robert Ramsay, who had a small shop in Sheffield where he sold pictures, plaster models, wood carvings, and such things. He was now in the midst of the things he loved, and he took great delight in handling pictures and plaster models. Nothing pleased him better than to model soft clay with his fingers. Sometimes a mould would be taken of a person's face, and young Chantrey thought that he would like to try and take a mould of this kind. He persuaded one of Mr. Ramsay's workmen to lie face upwards upon a table, and then he placed the soft plaster over the man's face and throat, and waited for it to harden. Suddenly the man rolled off the table and madly stripped away the plaster from his throat. Young Chantrey did not know that a man cannot breathe unless his throat can expand, and when this plaster began to harden it was making it impossible for the man to breathe.

He was so eager to gain knowledge that he rented a cheap little room, and spent his evenings and holidays drawing and making models. The long hours he spent in that room he never forgot, and in the year before he died he visited that little room, and spoke to friends of the many happy hours he had spent there.

When he was no longer an apprentice he looked around for some way in which to earn a living. He was severely handicapped in some ways. When he was ten years of age his parents made the discovery that he was quite blind in one eye. Up to that time no one had ever suspected such a thing. Then again he had attended school very little and was not by any means a good scholar. The letters which he wrote when he became a man show that even then he was a very poor scholar. His writing ran on without any punctuation; many words were wrongly spelt, and God was written with a small "g".

Those were the days when there were no photographers, and portrait painters could often make a fair living. Many artists went from farm to farm, seeking for work to do, and Francis Chantrey decided to do this. In 1802 he put the following advertisement in a Sheffield newspaper:

"Francis Chantrey begs permission to inform the ladies and gentlemen of Sheffield, and its vicinity, that, during his stay here, he wishes to employ his time in taking of portraits in crayons, and miniatures, at the pleasure of the person who shall do him the honour to sit. Although a young artist, he has had the opportunity of acquiring improvement from a strict attention to the works of Messrs. Smith, Arnold, gentlemen of eminence. He trusts in being happy to produce good and satisfactory likenesses; and no exertion shall be wanting on his part, to render his humble efforts deserving some small share of public patronage. Terms—from two to three guineas. 24 Paradise Square."

Chantrey was at this time twenty-one years of age. He worked hard at portrait-painting, and although he did not earn a great deal, he made a fair living. He painted shopkeepers, farmers and artisans. He painted a portrait of his old schoolmaster, Mr. Fox, and another of the vicar. The people of Norton Village were proud of him, and anxious to see him get a good start. At last he moved to London, and besides painting portraits he secured a position as a woodcarver's assistant. His total earnings were five shillings a day. For some time he had a very hard struggle. He was quite unknown and poor. It was only by taking care of every penny that he managed to live at all. In many ways these days were the hardest he had ever known, for he was all alone in London, and had to make his own way. He worked away at carving in a garret, and could only afford one candle, which he used to wear in his cap so that the light might move with him as he changed positions.

At this time the president of the Academy was the great painter, Benjamin West. Chantrey thought that if West would allow him to make a bust of him, it would do much to bring his work before the public, so he asked West to sit for a portrait in plaster. West was an unusually kind, but at the same time, a very busy man. He was at that time painting a great picture:

"Christ Healing the Sick." He told Chantrey that if he were willing to catch his likeness as he worked away at his picture, he was welcome to try. Chantrey was pleased with the offer and for many days he sat and moulded the plaster, as West worked at his task. The bust Chantrey did at this time can now be seen at the Royal Academy in London. Soon afterwards he made a bust of Mr. Samuel Shore, for which he received one hundred guineas; by far the largest sum he had ever been paid. He gave up painting altogether, for he was now fairly well established as a sculptor.

At that time there was living in London a very brilliant man, named Horn Tooke. Chantrey made a bust in plaster of this man and sent it to the exhibition. It looked at first as though there would not be a place for it there, but another sculptor, Mr. Joseph Nollekens, saw it and was much impressed. He was not jealous, but said: "This is a fine, a very fine bust; let the man who made it be known. Remove one of my busts and put it in its place, for it well deserves it." This was a great thing for Chantrey, for this bust aroused a great deal of interest, and he soon received commissions to do work which brought him more than twelve thousand pounds.

Very soon after this something happened which helped to bring Francis Chantrey more to the front than ever and to establish him as "The Prince of British Sculptors". In 1811 it was decided to erect a statue of King George III. Naturally there was a great deal of excitement among sculptors; all were anxious to receive the honour of doing it. A committee was formed to choose a sculptor. Fifteen of the greatest sculptors submitted designs to the committee, and the members decided that Chantrey's was the best, and so he was given the important task of doing it.

As soon as it was known that the commission had been given to Francis Chantrey, he had the news conveyed to his mother. He knew that it would give her great pleasure; and indeed it did, for she burst into tears. It seemed to her marvellous that her boy, who only a few years before had drawn pictures on the kitchen floor, should be chosen to design a statue of the king. There was great stir and excitement in the village of Norton. The wonderful tidings spread from cottage to cottage. "Francis Chantrey has been chosen to make the king's statue," was the news that everybody was repeating.

After making a statue of the king, of course, Chantrey was considered capable of making a design for any one, as indeed he was. The rich and famous crowded to his studio in order to get busts made of themselves. It would be impossible to put here a complete list of all for whom he made designs, but among other well-known people there were: Sir Walter Scott, Bishop Heber, who wrote "From Greenland's Icy Mountains" and other fine hymns; James Watt, the inventor, and many others.

Some years later, when William IV was king, Francis Chantrey was knighted, and so became Sir Francis Chantrey. After that brief reign came to an end, and George IV came to the throne, the monarch became a great admirer of Chantrey, and was so well pleased with the statue of himself, which the sculptor made, that he insisted on paying much more than had been agreed upon. This very fine statue now stands in Trafalgar Square, London, and for it Chantrey received the sum of nine thousand guineas. Magnificent statues done by Francis Chantrey may now be seen in many lands. In Ireland, Scotland, India, United States, and other lands his work is seen and appreciated.

His deep affection for his mother was shown in many ways. He loved to have her visit him at his home in London, and though she had been a humble, hard-working woman all her life, he was always proud to make her known to his friends. When, on one occasion he was very ill, he would not allow any one to acquaint his mother lest she should worry. The letters he wrote to his mother were full of tenderness and scarcely a week passed in which he did not send her some present.

He was modest to an extraordinary degree. Many men who have risen from lowly circumstances have become spoiled by success and made vain. Such was not the case with Francis Chantrey. He became the friend of great men and of kings, but he loved to talk of his humble origin, and fame never made him, in the least degree, vain.

Standing in the most crowded thoroughfare of London, England; in that square which has the Bank of England on the north, the Royal Exchange upon the east, the Mansion House on the south, with Cheapside running west, there stands a magnificent statue of the Duke of Wellington on horseback. Thousands have gazed upon that noble monument, and admired it. It is the work of Francis Chantrey. No doubt many who see it will think of a lonely little farmhouse, one hundred and fifty miles away, where he first saw the light, and they will remember the donkey boy who became the greatest of British sculptors.